*"The journey of a thousand miles
Begins with one step."*
Lao-Tse

"Just be sure you take that one step"
Bill O'Hearn

From The Heart Of A Lion
And Other Lessons To Sell By

Bill O'Hearn

ISBN: 0-9626161-1-7
Library of Congress Catalog Card Number: 92-074547

Entheos Publishing Company
P. O. Box 970
Wilsonville, Oregon 97070

Dedication

To my children, Molly, Patti, Julie and Chip, thank you from the bottom of my heart for turning out to be such fine human beings. Those times I missed being with you while you were growing up because of misplaced focus are acceptable only because of who you are today.

A Special Thanks To:

Thorn Bacon, my editor, whom I'm convinced uses more red ink than any editor around, but who still manages to convince me that I'm doing okay, and Ursula Bacon, who voluntarily kept her creative mind working to help bring this book to life.

Kathy Hove for her valuable assistance.

Bill Morreal, research associate for the Million Dollar round Table, for his considerable efforts and prompt response to my numerous requests for information.

Bill Conerly, of the Economics Department of The First Interstate Bank of Oregon, for providing me with charts, and teaching me how to use them, so I could, when appropriate, convert yesterday's dollars into today's dollars.

The staff of the Multnomah County Public Library general information department for their enthusiastic, friendly responses to my requests. May they count their blessings that I didn't learn of their great service during the early stages of this book.

Greg Hansen, Cliff Bailey, Roger Zener, Barney Rogers, Cheryl Matscheck, Cliff Canucci, Bruce Barnett, Lani O'Callaghan, Von Hansen, Al Sizer, Lee Gedeiko, Tom Wolff, and my daughter Molly for reviewing the manuscript, and being so generous with their time and ideas before we went to press.

Bob Steinberg for his valuable input which appears in this book, about a very special time in our lives.

My master mind group: Arthur Smith, Peter

Suriano, Cliff Canucci, and Lyle Nelson for their unconditional support.

Og Mandino, Larry Wilson, and Tom Wolff for their generous endorsements of this book. Their willingness to lend their name to my efforts means more to me than I can express.

All of you who became my clients, as well as friends, over the years. I don't know if I was luckier than other insurance agents, but let me tell you—I enjoyed our times together. You made the struggle of the early days all worthwhile. You are what a career is all about. You made this book possible.

A posthumous thank you, from the bottom of my heart, goes to my wife, Gloria, who was always there for me one hundred percent of the time. She helped me gain perspective with my successes and with my failures. My life was better because of her.

And finally, a thank you with love, to my special Elizabeth for her beautiful spirit and her dedication to making our present and our future so bright.

Author's Note

Throughout this book, as in my first book, *From the Heart of a Child and Other Lessons to Live By,* I struggled with the personal pronouns he and she. I finally decided to use the male gender for consistency. However, wherever appropriate, please realize I am referring to both.

Women were rarely involved in the sales forces of insurance companies when I started my career. Today, not only are they significant in numbers, they are noteworthy in their accomplishments.

I believe that the opportunity for women in the field of sales, especially in the life insurance industry, is absolutely unlimited, and that their natural abilities create a bonding with clients that many men could only hope for.

So please remember that I am speaking as much to women as I am to men. Thank you for your understanding.

Bill O'Hearn

Preface

"Ask not for victory, ask for courage.
For if you can endure you bring honor to us all,
Even more you bring honor to yourself."

From The Decathlon

The inspiration for the title of this book came from Cliff Canucci, a leading producer for Northwestern Mutual Life Insurance Company. He had just finished reading my first book, *From the Heart of a Child and Other Lessons to Live By*, when he telephoned me and said in an enthusiastic voice, "I have the title for your next book—*From the Heart of a Lion*."

From the Heart of a Lion—what an appropriate title for a book about to be written to the men and women of the sales profession.

Lions are rulers of their domain, monarchs of their circumstances. They are a symbol of courage and strength. Lions have *heart*. Aren't these the attributes needed to make it in the field of selling?

To all you who have demonstrated so ably the qualities of the lion hearted—the Tom Wolffs, the Ben Feldmans, the Jim Longleys, the Frank Sullivans, the John Todds and all the other sales greats from all fields—as well as to all of you who have stuck in there in spite of heartache, frustration and sometimes low commission checks—who may never be known to anyone except your families, friends and clients—thank you for your inspiration. Thank you for living *From the Heart of a Lion*.

Introduction

This is a book about success. It is also a book about failure. It is the story of the evolution of a sales person to a sales professional. It is my story.

More importantly, it is a story for you, a "How I did it" story to suggest "How you can do it better."

There is no ego involved here—at least I hope not. What is involved and what I hope comes through to you loud and clear is heart. I have felt for many years that the sales industry has failed to keep up with the times—not from a "high-tech" standpoint, but rather from a "high-touch" standpoint, to borrow a phrase from John Naisbitt's book, *Megatrends*. As our society moves faster and faster, less and less attention is being paid to balance in life. Many times the result of this acceleration is increased sales records and decreased quality of existence. There is a mentality among many companies that their business is sales and that the salesperson's personal life is not their concern. I disagree heartily. I believe that as companies pay more and more attention to the overall well-being of their sales force, they will see dramatic increases in productivity.

But I am not writing this book for the companies, although I hope they take note. I am writing this book for you, the professional sales person or manager. In the end, it will be you who benefits from any knowledge I can share with you. And that will benefit everyone.

The book follows my career from its beginning through all the stages of growth for over forty years. I wrote it from my perspective with the hope that the lessons I learned, and the lessons I failed to learn, will stand out clearly as a beacon to guide you on your path to success.

The journey of life is meant to be an adventure. I have always believed that when you choose to take control of your destiny, you have the opportunity to design whatever adventure, whatever life, you desire.

So, this book is really about life. My life—in the hope that it will touch your life. If it does, then you will touch the lives of others, and experience the essence of what being here on earth is all about.

Table of Contents

" *Climb high*
  Climb far
    Your goal is the sky
      Your aim is the star. "

Inscription on Hopkins Memorial Steps
Williams College

CHAPTER 1

A Journey Of A Thousand Miles

It was June, 1949. I had just graduated from the University of Oregon and I didn't have the foggiest idea of what my lifetime career should be. All I knew is that I had to get a job. Up to this point, my experience had consisted of delivering clothes for a dry cleaner, digging ditches for the city, selling ladies shoes, being a section hand for the railroad, a cannery worker, a carpenter's helper and a forest service worker. All were summer jobs, and none gave me a clue about what I might like to do with my life, although they had taught me what I didn't want to do—even though I was pretty good at selling ladies shoes and handbags.

I had grown up in Eugene, Oregon where the University of Oregon is located, but decided upon graduation and marriage to my sweetheart, Gloria Aguer, that sunny southern California held my pot of gold. I lasted four months. I was used to smiling, friendly people, something I wasn't seeing, so we packed up our few belongings and moved to what was to be our home town for the next 35 years, Albany, Oregon.

During the two and a half years after graduation I held six jobs, most of them in sales. I sold men's clothing, sporting goods, and major appliances. I also spent some time working for a credit reporting firm collecting bad debts. Also during this time, I took an aptitude test for selling life insurance, as a lark, three different times for three different companies. I passed with flying colors. One test I took with The Prudential, in Eugene, after returning from California, but I decided against going with them because I didn't want to hand in a list of 100 friends who might be prospects. I felt uneasy about the idea of, as I saw it, imposing on my friends.

Mutual of New York and its General Agent, Oscar Specht, who was based in Salem, 25 miles from Albany, said I passed the test with the highest grade ever recorded in the agency, however, they felt that at age 23 I was just too young. That and the fact that I had a net worth of approximately zero. It kind of made me mad.

Finally, at age 25, I knew I had to make some career decisions. The retail business was easy to eliminate. I didn't like working on Saturdays. And, I didn't want to work for a big corporation. I kind of felt that to them I was just a number without a name.

About this time, my friend, Dr. Arne Jensen, recommended me to New York Life. They wrote me a nice letter and asked me to drive 50 miles to come see them. It seemed to me that if they were interested in me, they should have driven the fifty miles to see me. Little ego problem there.

As a result of the New York Life letter, I went to

see a great human being, Raymond Fisher, whom I had
gone to earlier for advice about the property and casualty
insurance business. He suggested I join him if I was
considering life insurance as a career. His main business
was with property and casualty, although he couldn't use
me there, but he did sell life insurance, too. Because of his
solid reputation, the life insurance company he
represented, Western Life Insurance Company of Helena,
Montana, didn't even test me, and they offered me $300 a
month as a draw against future commissions.

I had a tough decision to make because at the same
time a car agency asked me to come to work for them.
They were offering a $475 a month salary, *plus*
commissions, *and* a new Buick Roadmaster to drive as a
demonstrator. I faced one of my most important learning
experiences in life.

Opportunity Versus Security

Did I want the security of a guaranteed income, (the
Buick agency), or was I willing to bet on myself in
exchange for opportunity? Did I have what it would take to
make it in the insurance business? Did I believe in myself
enough? The risk seemed immense. What if I tried and
didn't make it?

On the other hand, while there didn't appear to be
much risk in selling cars, the future seemed limited. I
couldn't imagine how I could ever end up owning an
automobile dealership. The amount of money it would take
seemed impossible, no matter how good I might be at
selling cars.

Financially, $300 a month was as close to
starvation wages as you could get. How badly did I want

opportunity? In fact, what did I think the opportunity actually was? I finally reached the point where I was helpless. I had been chewing on this problem for almost two months and I could not make a decision. I had talked to my folks and they would be supportive which ever way I decided. I talked to my doctor friend who had recommended me to New York Life. He was positive for a try at insurance. Most everyone else was pretty unanimous for the car business. "Who would ever want to sell life insurance?" was their question. But something kept nagging at me. There was opportunity in the insurance business. I had been told that I could become as successful as I allowed myself to be. The pivotal issue became this:

> *Did I want to be my own boss, or did I want to work for someone else? Did I want my future to be in my hands or in someone else's?*

Finally, the day of reckoning came, I could put off the decision no longer. I promised myself I would not go to bed this particular night until I had made up my mind.

As coincidence would have it, my brother-in-law, Tom Aguer, was starting college at this very time to become a pharmacist and at three o'clock in the morning my rationale finally became this: If Tommy could struggle through school for five years to become a pharmacist, I could struggle through the life insurance business for five years to learn how to sell insurance. I promised myself that night that I would absolutely not question my decision for five years. By the end of that time the evidence would be in. It was a life-changing promise. Had I merely said I would "try" the life insurance business, I never would have made it as you will see in the next chapter.

Reflections

*A*s I look back over the years since my decision to go into the insurance business I understand now that I had chosen between two options: instant gratification as a car salesman, with a nice new car and more money, or delayed gratification—the possibility for greater gains in the long run—as a life insurance agent.

My decision to enter insurance was a major victory over my selfish self who wanted it *now*, by my more courageous self who was willing to take a risk. It was a victory over fear of the unknown. This quote, from an unknown source, was to become a favorite of mine:

"Fear knocked. I answered. No one was there."

*"Destiny is no matter of chance.
It is a matter of choice:
It is not a thing to be waited for,
It is a thing to be achieved."*

William Jennings Bryan

CHAPTER 2

The First
Step

And so it began. Western Life had no training program and Raymond Fisher's real expertise was in the property and casualty business. Raymond did a good job for Western Life, but most of his sales came about as a result of his rapport with his property and casualty clients. The net result was that he could not really give me a sales track to run with, or really teach me how to prospect—something I would have had with New York Life. However, I was satisfied that I had made the right decision so I just studied whatever I could find, and asked Raymond lots of questions. He was always there for me and gave me great moral support, but I was about to find out what survival against the odds was all about.

I did have three things going for me. I had tremendous enthusiasm, great energy, and liked people. I also had something going against me. I absolutely hated rejection. Obviously, my enthusiasm knew some bounds.

There was one important aspect of the life insurance business that I was not to understand for several years. Even though I had selected opportunity versus security, I did not understand that I had gone into business for myself. All of the jobs I had held previously were pretty much situations that required reaction instead of action. I waited until a customer came in and then I started to sell, or I waited until a bad bill came in when I was a debt collector and began to collect—sometimes. Nothing I had done prepared me for any more discipline than getting up and going to work on time—and leaving my work behind me at the end of the day. I really had no concept of being totally responsible for my own future. Because of the $300 a month draw I still acted like a salaried employee. I now call it the *illusion of the draw.*

A draw against future commissions is very different than a guarantee plus a percentage. The latter keeps you on a salary with some incentive to do more. The former merely gives the illusion of being on a salary with incentive only to meet your draw. You are borrowing money against your ability to produce which is fine if that gives you a sense of urgency. The problem with me was that it felt like a salary. In other words:

Money Came In No Matter What I Did

I had no sense of urgency. I knew I was going to receive $300 at the beginning of every month—and in return I was to learn how to sell insurance by going out and getting my nose bloodied. There were a few barriers. I had no concept of:

Prospecting
Management of time
How to approach a prospect
Use of the telephone
The fact finding interview
The presentation
The close
The follow up
Clients versus Customers
and
The power of goals

I understood just two things. I had a commitment to the life insurance business for five years, and I had $300 a month coming in to keep the wolves from the door. The $300 a month I really understood. That meant survival. What the "five year commitment" part meant I didn't have a clue.

Reflections

There were so many reasons for me not to make it in the business of selling life insurance. Trying to convince a prospect to spend $5.00 a month to protect his family in case of his death, and failing most of the time to do so, was not exactly an uplifting experience. It took me a while to understand that I was not talking to a good prospect for my product when I heard, "I'm not going to leave money so some other guy can come along and spend it if I die." I was talking to someone who didn't really care about the same things I did.

The idea of leaving Gloria without some basic way to survive financially, at least for a while, was absolutely not acceptable to me. I only owned $10,000 of G.I. insurance and $10,000 of permanent insurance, which was a little over $100,000 in today's dollars, but at least that spoke to my beliefs.

I can't put all the blame on my prospects though. Other than for an intuitive feeling, even I didn't understand all the reasons for owning insurance. Between my lack of understanding and my prospect's rejection of life insurance, I sure didn't accomplish much.

Eventually I began to understand that the purchase of life insurance is a character buy, but in those early days I just kept banging my head against the wall.

The lesson I hope you will take away from my experience is this:

The prospects you seek must be able to:
- *Recognize there is a problem,*
- *Have a basic desire to solve that problem, and*
- *Have the money to pay for the solution.*

"*Our doubts are traitors,*
And make us lose the good
We oft might win
By fearing to attempt."

William Shakespeare

CHAPTER 3

Early Wanderings

Moving to the town of Albany proved to be a good decision. It was small and friendly. Even though we had been there a little over two years, we still did not know very many people. I had been told this would be a disadvantage in starting my insurance practice, but I didn't view it that way. I had no intention of calling on friends anyway. However, my very first sale was to Arne Jensen, the friend who had mentioned me to New York Life. He came to me and said he wanted a small policy on one of his daughters. I probably never told Arne this, but that act of friendship gave me the boost I needed to prove that people actually would buy my product. And he continued to support me by becoming one of my biggest clients over the years.

Notice how that word "clients" sneaked in there? That was a word I was not going to use for a few years because I still had no idea of what the life insurance business, or any selling business, was all about. I thought it was a game in which I had to convince someone to talk to me about something he didn't want to talk about, and buy something he really didn't want to buy. You couldn't accuse me of having missionary zeal in my new job.

According to the sign on the highway, our town had about 6,000 residents. My sole job was to start finding someone, anyone, to talk to. I had no sales skills, no telephone skills, no prospecting skills and I didn't even know there were such things as closing skills—a fact I was to prove over and over.

I can't remember how I came up with the idea, but I picked up a copy of our city directory from the Chamber of Commerce and it became my primary prospecting tool. In those days the directory listed the names of the entire family and gave the ages of the children. Even though Gloria and I had no children yet, I figured that anyone with children under age six might be close to my own age. Someone with a ten-year-old child would obviously be an old codger and not in my league. I filled out a three by five card on every family that qualified under my guidelines and started my new life.

I decided to call at the home of these "prospects" instead of telephoning them. I think subconsciously I had figured out that I couldn't talk to as many people in person as on the phone and that, in my mind, meant fewer rejections. Little did I realize that there was no way to reduce the number of rejections necessary to make one sale. And I soon found out that rejection in person is even more unpleasant than rejection over the phone.

Can you imagine the joy of getting up each morning knowing that you are going to get to knock on the doors of dozens of strangers that day? Had I not made the irrevocable "Five-Year Promise" I never could have kept on. It was not that I was unaccustomed to knocking on doors. When I was twelve years old, I was a crackerjack newspaper delivery boy and part of my job was to get new subscriptions. I can still remember how I would knock on a door and then make my little sales talk in what I thought was a southern accent. For reasons I can't remember, I figured that the ladies who answered the door would take more kindly to a sweet southern boy trying to make his way by selling papers. It must have been something I picked up from some movie. Whatever the reason, I was successful. I won a beautiful Schwinn bicycle, with balloon tires and knee-action, for my efforts. However, my newspaper experience didn't make knocking on doors for insurance any easier. I think it was about this time that I began to create one of the several limiting myths that were to become part of my world, and it was this:

> *If I was just six foot-one and had a southern accent I could really sell!*

The funny part was that I really believed that. But I wasn't six foot-one, I was five foot-eleven, and I didn't have a southern accent. What had worked when I was 12 wouldn't work at age 25. I wanted no part of being a huckster, but it did give me one more excuse for failing.

So I just kept knocking on doors and met the strangest mix of people. I met them only long enough to get a "no." I can't really remember making one appointment although I'm sure I must have. I can remember one lady who disappeared from her door when I told her I was a life insurance man. She reappeared a moment later and began to read the red, underlined parts from her Bible about how the Lord provideth. What a lecture. I felt as if I was back in the fifth grade with one of the Catholic nuns giving me an embarrassing scolding for talking in class. I can't remember if the lady thought I was from the devil or just a poor unenlightened soul, but I do remember not wanting to make any more calls that day.

Besides, how did she know I was coming to her home—having the exact parts underlined in red and all?

Reflections

*A*t this stage in my life I had absolutely no *vision*. I had a survival mentality. It didn't occur to me to step outside of myself and try to imagine what I might accomplish. Just trying to accomplish the minimum was almost more than I could imagine.

I wonder how many times in life we all accept limiting imagination without giving it much thought?

In my studies of how to make myself perform more towards my potential over the years, I discovered that most scientists dealing with human behavior believe that approximately 85 percent of the pictures we hold in our imagination are negative. How can we possibly hope to tap our inner power when most of the time we are watching the B-movies of our mind?

As a regular exercise, I urge you to stop, step outside yourself, and just let your positive, creative imagination take a fling at what it thinks might be possible. What others call daydreaming, I refer to as designing your future. It can be very productive time.

Remember, the same kind of thinking that got you where you are today, will probably not get you where you want to be tomorrow. So, once in awhile, call time out and see what kind of strange and wondrous ideas might be knocking at the door. You might discover a pleasant surprise.

Don't be afraid to dream big dreams.

"*It is not who you think you are*
That is holding you back—
It is who you think you are not. "

Anonymous

"*How can I believe there is a*
Butterfly in you or me, when all
I can see is a fuzzy worm. "

excerpt from
Hope for the Flowers
Trina Paulus

CHAPTER 4

Myths To Fail By

Discouraged because I was not making any sales, miserable because I disliked calling on people who didn't want to talk to me, out of desperation I did what every sales person should do. I went to the leading life insurance producer in our town and cried, "Help!"

Raymond Fisher had been totally supportive in every way possible, but I needed the perspective of someone who did nothing but sell life insurance. So I went to Bert Harger.

Bert was a veteran insurance man with the Atlas Life Insurance Company who could do two things better than anyone I ever met: He could knock on doors of strangers, and he could sell lots of policies. While most of the new and established agents in the area would each eventually end up writing 40 or 50 cases a year, Bert had a track record several years long of over 150 sales a year.

Because he knocked on so many doors he carried a smooth stone to knock with to save the skin on his knuckles. He was not only in another league, he was in another world.

And he was willing to help me in any way he could. As it turned out, I didn't learn any particular selling skills, but what I did get was the inspiration that there were all kinds of people out there willing to listen to me if I had something interesting to say—and if I was willing to say it often enough. My approach up to this point must have been, "You don't wanna buy life insurance do you?"

So I began to search for something interesting to say. Even though I had only been in the business for eight months, I enrolled in Part Two of LUTC (Life Underwriters Training Council). It was being offered in Salem, and was a six-month course on how to sell advanced cases. It would have been nice to take a course on how to sell unadvanced cases first, but it wasn't being offered that year. I was going at it backwards, but I was willing to do whatever was necessary to become as successful as Bert Harger.

About this time Raymond suggested that I join the Life Underwriters Association which was just starting in our three-town area. I became its first secretary. It gave me some extra duties to do besides calling on people, which was okay by me. And it did introduce me to a few more top producers—and a bunch more like me.

My first very unsuccessful year was coming to a close and I hadn't even validated the $300 a month draw. That meant I owed the company money, so I did what must come naturally to a sales person: I asked Western Life for a bigger draw. And with this experience I learned another principle which was to stand me in good stead in the art of selling:

If you don't ask—you don't receive.

I needed at least $350 a month just to get by. Any sensible person could see that I was not making it, but I convinced Raymond and he convinced Western Life. I think they said yes because Raymond guaranteed it. Now I had to go to work in earnest—whatever that meant. However, Christmas was coming up and I was again making plans to work at Merrill's Clothing Store to earn some Christmas money—and to reaffirm another myth I had invented:

Nobody buys insurance in December!

This myth went along with several other thoughts I had developed which in retrospect I now call:

Myths To Fail By

If they are breathing, aren't making much money and are close to my age, I've got a prospect.

I can only talk to people in my own age and income bracket.

I can't work any harder because people will only see me at night, and I'm working four nights a week now.

I have to work five days and four nights a week just to survive.

No one likes to refer an insurance man to his friends, so there is no use asking for referred leads.

I have to call on 21 prospects to get four interviews, and I have to have four interviews to get one sale.

I keep good records and numbers never lie. Therefore, I would have to work 16 nights a week to sell a million dollars of insurance.

So I went to work at Merrill's for the holiday season. After all, a guy's got to earn some money somehow.

Reflections

*"Hell would be—
If God were to show me the things
I could have accomplished
If only I had believed in myself."*

Anonymous

*I*t is so interesting to me now to look back on how many "truths," also known as "myths," I developed about what I had to do to sell insurance and what I believed was the extent of my talent. My verbal assessment of my skills and abilities was unabashed. I could really talk a good game. However, my mental assessment of myself put lid after lid on my performance. My observations in the years that followed have led me to believe that most salespeople do the same thing.

Take a look at your situation. Are you placing lids on what you could accomplish? You might answer that you are doing the very best you know how, and I would have to ask you if that answer might in itself be a lid. I've asked myself at different times in my life, "What would you do if you knew you couldn't fail?" Each time I realized that I would do something more than I was doing. So why don't you recognize the myths you have manufactured—or someone else has manufactured for you? Part of it is because you probably don't recognize what is really true and what isn't. You may have established from your records that your closing ratio is one out of three. If you had been able to walk up to that great life insurance salesman John Savage, before he passed away, and suggest that closing one sale out of every three interviews was a pretty good truth to operate by he might've wanted to have a heart-to-heart talk with you.

So what is it going to take for you to change and grow? The very first thing I believe you must do, and maybe the most important, is to examine the feelings behind your "truths." Do these feelings contain any element of fear? Is it possible you may be afraid you would fail if you were to challenge your truths? Pretty human reaction, but here is where it is important for you to risk. The chances are, if you are going to grow, that you will be replacing your current truths on a regular basis.

So my wish for you is that you keep striving to take the lid off your thinking—that you examine as objectively as you can what you could really do if you believed differently. If you find it difficult to do this, then ask someone who really cares about you and your career what he or she thinks your potential is. And remember, even that opinion is a lid. But it might be a better lid than the one you are operating under now. You'll find excitement and new adventures in learning if you will do this.

Go for it!

Always believe that anything is possible.

*"It is in your moments of decision
That your destiny is shaped."*

Anthony Robbins

CHAPTER 5

A Lack Of Vision

I spent the next three years pretending to be a professional insurance man. I even started my CLU (Chartered Life Underwriter) studies. But even though the class was 45 miles away, the time I spent driving, and learning, was a respite from making calls on people who didn't want to buy what I had to offer. Besides, I figured a salesman who had an advanced certification in his profession would earn some respect. Was it possible that I was studying to help my ego rather than to learn? I think a little bit of both. However, had I known at the time that it was going to take nine years to get my designation I might have been too discouraged to start.

About this time I discovered that the Purdue Life Insurance Marketing Institute had devised a guideline of efforts and results for the agents in the field based upon reported results from Institute graduates. What came out of their extensive research was a series of numbers, 20-10-2-

20, called the Purdue Formula. Thanks to Daniel Alexandre, of the Life Insurance Agency Management Association, here is an excerpt from an article in the Purdue Life News of November 25, 1949.

"These numbers (20-10-2-20) represent the weekly activities each and every man must follow; 20 "seen calls" per week, wherein the agent spends at least 10 minutes in front of a prospect, shooting for an interview; 10 closing interviews, wherein the agent asks the prospect to buy at least six times before giving up; 2 apps, which will give the agent a selling ratio of five interviews to one app; and finally, 20 new, good, qualified prospects to start all over again the next week."

The Purdue Formula was the definitive study in the insurance industry at this time, and I figured if I followed it I couldn't miss. The article continued:

"Since these statistics were compiled, another study has revealed the following facts: 1. The leaders in every class consistently do the following facts: 20-10-2-20, or better, each and every week. 2. The marginal or average producers are operating very near what the formula calls for. 3. The men who are off schedule and having the greatest difficulties are those who are failing to approach the efforts required of the formula."

I had kept meticulous work effort records and this is what my records showed for the year before.

Calls per week	21
Closing Interviews per week	4
Sales per week	1

Anyone could look at my results and determine that I was in category #3. So I decided to pick up the pace a bit.

I made a commitment to forty calls a week. I did not make a commitment to spend ten minutes in front of twenty prospects, or secure ten interviews, or ask the prospect to buy six times, or make more sales—just a commitment to make more calls. In other words, I was going to make calls just for the record—and I was naive enough to believe I had the answer to success. However, this was the truth that emerged:

Making calls without a personal commitment to secure appointments will only give you more calls, not more appointments.

I deluded myself into believing I was doing things right. Finally, after about 8 weeks in a row of 40 calls with no improvement in results, I became discouraged enough to let myself fall right back into my old habits. Twenty calls a week—and continued failure.

I still had no clue as to what I had to do to make my career work except to tell myself that if I wanted to double my production I would have to work eight nights a week. So I kept scratching and clawing to survive. I was at an impasse.

The irresistible force had met the immovable object.

The catalyst for my failure could be narrowed down to one word: Fear. Plain and simple, the fear of rejection. I had a very thin skin. I was still at an age and time in my life when I wanted everyone to like me and believed that they would if they only knew me (another myth). In other words:

My vision of success was not great enough to offset the pain of rejection.

The fear of rejection was an emotion that was stronger than my motivation to succeed. I did lots of things to avoid actions which would result in pain. I mowed the lawn in the middle of the day. I'd be "too tired" to make another call. I'd bury myself in my studies which took up time and got me out of the line of fire. I would drive right by a prospect's house if the blinds were pulled or if I didn't see a car parked in the driveway because, "They probably aren't home anyway."

Intellectually, I understood that a "no" wasn't a personal rejection. And intellectually I understood that I had to get so many "no's" in order to get one "yes." And I understood that Babe Ruth had more strikeouts than anyone in professional baseball, but also had more home runs. I understood all that intellectually. Emotionally though, I was in kindergarten.

But change had to come. Western Life had been more than generous, but I sensed that even they were wondering if I would ever turn the corner. They knew that, on a national average, only one out of five new agents is still around after five years. I had only one year left of my commitment to not look back for five years, and was one year away from becoming a statistic when a force came into play that I had not yet been exposed to—EGO. Was I really going to fail in the insurance business? And if I did, how could I expect to succeed in anything else? I felt I had what it took, but the records held the proof. I was not making it. I owed the insurance company $2700, some of which might be offset by renewals, but it still looked like an enormous debt to me.

And then one of those seemingly common events resulted in a life changing decision.

One day I was meeting with a great guy, Bob Cummins, sales vice-president for Standard Insurance Company. We had talked a couple of times over the years about my coming with his company because he believed that in spite of my record I had the talent to be a million dollar producer. So did I—kind of. He never told me what it was he saw in me but his conviction seemed unshakeable. My belief in myself had been reduced by four years of disappointment. To become a million dollar producer I would have to become one of only forty out of more than 6,000 life insurance agents in the State of Oregon who reached that magical mark each year.

It was October, and if I stayed on schedule, I would end the year with about a quarter of a million in sales. That was on about a par with other new agents in Oregon, but then again most of us wouldn't make it. Even though one year I had done a bit better, it seemed that my limit was $250,000. Four years of effort to sell a little over one million dollars of insurance. And Bob Cummins believed I could do that in one year? Come on!

But as he drove away in his big, beautiful, black Lincoln Continental (and the picture of him is as clear today in my mind, 35 years later, as it was then), I thought about my small, brown and not too beautiful Volkswagen Beetle and my debt and my direction. I became disgusted with myself. And as I stood there watching Bob's car disappear I said, "Bill, you are either as good as you keep saying you could be—or you're not. It's time to put up or shut up." At that moment, I became a million dollar producer.

Sure I still had to learn how, which meant

shattering the myths I had developed over the past four years. And I needed a couple of months to build up my intestinal fortitude before making the decision public. If I was really serious, which I was, I figured the best thing I could do was to announce to the world (my world) my intentions. If that didn't put the pressure on me to perform nothing would. And I still had to face the butterflies flying in formation in my stomach every morning when I awoke to the thought of, "How in the world can I find anyone to buy life insurance?" But I was committed. Somehow, someway, in my fifth full year in the insurance business, I must find a way to join the top-ranked insurance producers in Oregon.

Results became more important than the rejections. The goal was cast in concrete. The method seemed cast in molasses.

Reflections

*O*ften I have looked back and wondered what forces were at work to make me change my attitude about succeeding. I always wanted to succeed. That was never a question. It seems, in retrospect, that my motivation to do whatever it took was missing in those first four years.

I didn't know what the price of success was but it seemed enormous. I kept telling myself that I wasn't afraid of hard work, and that was true. But a little voice kept whispering inside me: "What if you do whatever it takes, whatever that is, and it doesn't work? What if you make that enormous effort and fail?" The thought of putting out all that effort and not having the expected results was a real roadblock.

I could have stayed in that mediocre mode of thinking all of my life, but I must have had a guardian angel pushing me. Maybe Bob Cummins was my guardian angel in disguise. Or maybe my guardian angel was pushing him. I just don't know.

What I do know is that for reasons beyond me I went—in the blink of a thought—from failure to success.

What about you? Is there some rationalization that is keeping you from realizing your dreams? Is the procrastination side of your nature keeping you from making decisions right now that would change the course of your entire life? This question is not just for you readers who haven't hit your stride yet. It is also for those of you who are proud of what you have accomplished, but are sitting on a plateau, resting on your laurels.

There is so much more out there to be experienced. All it takes is a flash of insight into who you really can be, and a no-holds-barred decision to go for it. Who knows—maybe your guardian angel is pushing and pulling. Listen close. Pay attention. There is more to you than you realize.

Every once in awhile take a quantum leap
in your thinking—it is scary and exciting, and
it's what life is all about.

"If one advances confidently
In the direction of his dreams,
And endeavors to live the life
Which he has imagined,
He will meet with a success
Unexpected in common hours."

Henry David Thoreau

CHAPTER 6

The Turning Point

As Thoreau said, once the path is determined all kinds of things begin to happen. My first decision was to again seek the help of an expert. This expert, Jim Metzker, was a million dollar producer from a neighboring town. Jim and I had studied some of the CLU courses together and had become friends. I can still recall asking him several times during my unsuccessful years, "How do you write a million dollars of insurance?" He always gave me answers that told me what he did. I could not at that time picture myself calling on the kind of prospects Jim did. After all, he knew what to say, he was older than I was and he could talk to people with money because he made money. Only when I finally asked him "How can 'I' write a million?" did I get on the right track.

I told Jim that I had set my sights, with no-holds-barred, on million dollar production in the coming year, and asked if he would help me figure out how to reach that goal. He asked me to let him examine my records from the previous four years. I was pleased that I had been so diligent in at least that one important area. Here are copies of actual record cards I gave to Jim Metzker to show him my weekly and monthly work effort—if that's what you could call it.

WEEK ENDING MAY 7, 1955

DAY	STUDY	OFFICE	FIELD	TOTAL HOURS	SEEN CALLS	INT	INS	PREM
MON	3½	3½	2	9	1	1		
TUES	1	2½	5½	9	9	2	12,000 12,000	119 $\frac{76}{16}$ 110 $\frac{16}{}$
WED	1	3½	3½	8	5	—		
THURS	1	1½	½	3	2	—		
FRI	1	2½	2½	6	5	1		
SAT	5½			5½				
TOTAL	13	13½	14	40½	22	4	24,000	229 $\frac{92}{}$

MONTH OF MAY, 1955
SUMMARY SHEET

TOTAL HOURS	167½	EACH HOUR	1.93
FIELD	65	EACH CALL	3.25
OFFICE	59½	EACH INT	16.25
STUDY	43	EACH SALE	81.25
TOTAL CALLS	100	TIME IN FIELD	5.00
INTERVIEWS	20	CLOSING RATIO	1-5
SALES	4	$29,000 VOLUME	
PREMIUM	648 $\frac{96}{}$		
ANN COMM	324 $\frac{48}{}$		

Even I could look at the cards and see what I had to do. Simple. Just work sixteen nights a week. It didn't take a genius to figure that out. Jim, however, looked at my results from a different perspective. He said, "It is obvious that all you have to do to write a million is to increase the number of your interviews and your average size case." I knew that to increase my number of interviews I would have to make more calls. I wasn't concerned about that because the prospect of working harder than I had ever done in my life was already a foregone conclusion. What I didn't know was how to find the time to have more interviews since my nights were already filled with appointments. Jim said that I would just have to find some daytime interviews and that would go along with his second observation that I would need to raise my average size case. He said that if I would call on some businessmen I would create bigger sales. Figuring out how to do that was up to me. But what he said made sense, even if I had no idea how to implement the program. At least I began to think in terms of where I might find more and better prospects to ask to buy my product.

Then the first of many "coincidences" happened. I don't remember how, but a book by a man named Frank Bettger called, *How I Raised Myself from Failure to Success in Selling,* appeared in my life (Frank's book is still available, and is published by Prentice Hall. I urge you to read it. You'll find inspiration, just as I did).

Have you ever heard the saying "When the student is ready, the teacher will appear?" Frank Bettger's book was to offer that extra step so few books contained. Most books will tell you what to do—be enthusiastic, have a great attitude, be organized. I already owned the attitude and enthusiasm part, but this book told me how to get organized.

One page in his book showed record cards similar to the one I had devised and had used for the past four years. On the next page, however, was a "Weekly Time Table" Here is what I remember it looked like. (See page 43)

I decided that if I was going to have to be better organized than I ever had been in my life, why not just adopt Frank Bettger's plan. It was simple. It had worked for him. I would make it work for me.

Bettger's book gave me one other great idea. If I was going to reach my goal, not only would I have to be more organized than I was before, I was also going to have to set aside enough time to actually think through what I needed to do, and when I was going to do it. Up to this point in my career, I had found that writing out the list of prospects I intended to see for the week was not too difficult. Most weeks, however, I worked off the previous week's list since my work effort was not exactly inspired. Actually calling on the names I had written down had been a hit or miss procedure.

What I now decided to do was to emulate the method of an insurance man named Richard Campbell, mentioned in Frank Bettger's book. Richard took every Friday and planned the entire next week. I can't imagine how I brought myself to make such a decision. There was nothing in the world—except making cold calls—I disliked more than sitting down to be an accountant type and making plans. I didn't like to call on people and I didn't like taking time to be organized. I guess my attitude needed a little fine tuning.

However, my attitude was to change with my new-found burning vision of who I was to become. Getting organized was to turn out to be the hardest work I had ever

	Monday	Tuesday	Wednesday	Thursday	Friday
M O R N I N G					
N O O N					
A F T E R N O O N					
E V E N I N G					

done—ever. More on that later.

So December 31, 1956 came and with it the end of the first phase of my insurance career. Four years and three months of the worst paid easy work in the world. A period in which my only commitment had been to survive the five year trial. At the end of four years and three months of struggle I was $2,700 in debt to my draw and had sold slightly over $1,000,000 dollars of insurance for the entire time.

You see, I had thought I was in the insurance business to sell insurance. I didn't realize I was there to build dreams and to make dreams come true, not only for others, but also for me. I didn't realize that I could touch the lives of others and in doing so touch the lives of myself and my family. I didn't realize I had talent just waiting for direction. I didn't realize the power of written-down goals. I didn't realize the need for making choices and taking risks. I didn't realize that my destiny was in my hands. I didn't realize that selling could be the best paid hard work in the world and I sure didn't realize that:

"If one advances confidently in the direction of his dreams..."

But I was about to find out.

Reflections

*T*here is a principle which took me a long time to learn, and which, even today, I will sometimes forget—often to my detriment. I would like to share it with you since I believe that understanding this principle, and taking advantage of it, can have a major influence on your life.

If I remember correctly, it was Ralph Waldo Emerson who talked about this principle in his essays. I believe he called it the "Law of Radiation and Attraction." In effect it means that whatsoever you radiate by virtue of your thoughts, attitudes and actions, is what you are going to attract. In other words, you are always radiating whether you mean to or not.

That can be good news or bad news. Unfortunately, is it often bad news because when you don't choose what you radiate, you frequently attract what you really don't want. In other words:

No choice is a choice and
no decision is a decision.

If you are not working towards an exciting goal, the odds are you are, by default, working towards an unexciting goal.

If the Law of Radiation and Attraction is valid,

and I believe it is, don't you think it would be a good move to sit down and do some serious goal setting in each area of your life? It is called picking what you want to radiate. It is called taking control of your future. Sounds like a good idea to me. How does it sound to you?

Make your choices on purpose—not by default.

*"The greatest discovery of my generation
Is that a human being can alter his life
By altering his attitudes of mind."*

William James

CHAPTER 7

An
Overview

Before we go on to the results of my fifth year, let's see if in retrospect I can share with you some insight into what was at the core of my failing year after year.

I graduated from college at age 22, got married immediately, and we went to work. Gloria became a secretary and I went to work as a salesman in a men's clothing store. We had two incomes, both marginal. In fact, I had accepted the job at the clothing store for $150 a month—a hundred below the market—to have what I thought was a great opportunity to learn the clothing business. How wrong I was, but that is a different story. Then, I had various selling or people-related jobs until I went into the insurance business when I was 25.

I had Raymond Fisher teach me what he knew, and I had LUTC, and Bert Harger. Agents going with companies like New York Life had pretty formalized training tracks. My training track was going out and getting my nose bloodied. Regardless of formal training or not I think that even today most new agents coming into the insurance business or any other commission selling business are still not taught the most important ingredient of selling. In other words, they are taught:

How to sell
not
Why to sell

I will go into that in a later chapter, but for now let's just settle on the fact that I did not have a clear idea of "why" I was in the insurance business. Sure, I knew such words as opportunity and being my own boss, and freedom. I just had no idea what that meant. And in my mind today, without a "why" any of us in sales will eventually fail. You can only sell so many widgets before you lose interest. A sales life must have meaning. I didn't understand that. To put it simply:

I had no dreams,
and
I had no vision.

In retrospect, I realize now that my real motivation was survival, even minimal survival. Make enough money to pay the bills and maybe take a vacation once a year. That is not freedom—that is slavery—self imposed. That makes for an existence instead of a life.

So what changed to take me from failure to success as society measures it? My first real goal is what changed me. My first real goal elevated my purpose beyond survival. I HAD to become a million dollar producer. The times are innumerable that I have silently thanked the insurance industry's Million Dollar Round Table for providing a yardstick. It gave me a definable goal—a mark to shoot for. A sign of success—or at least a path to success. Not since I decided years earlier to become an Eagle Scout had I felt the direction and vision that becoming a member of the Million Dollar Round Table gave me.

Those 32 great visionaries, who, in 1927, gathered at the Peabody Hotel in Memphis, Tennessee and put their energies into forming the MDRT, touched the lives of thousands like me. Thank you wherever you are.

I still hadn't discovered the much deeper path to success in life. But I was going to have the opportunity to meet some of those who had.

So as I started my fifth year, I had determination and a mind set that swept aside all excuses. I would write a million dollars of insurance this year. Period. No question about it. Just stand aside, 'cause I'm coming through. Keep in mind that I did not make this decision for all the right reasons. In fact, the underlying force came from my having to prove that I was O.K. I'm sure psychologists could find a name for this, but the point was that the time had come for Bill O'Hearn to prove to himself, and I know that I hoped others would agree, that he was a winner and not a loser. As Anthony Robbins, author of *Unlimited Power* and *Awaken the Giant Within*, might say today, the pain of staying in the grip of mediocrity became too great. I had to change.

Little did I know that my whole life would take on a different meaning and that my decision would forever change the direction of me and my family—and influence the lives of people I didn't even know yet.

Reflections

*D*uring the early years I remember thinking a great deal about a quote by Cus D'Amato, the famous fight manager: "A professional is someone who does what he knows he has to do no matter how he feels inside."

It seems that I was constantly struggling to do what I didn't want to do, and not winning the battle most of the time.

Have you ever experienced the same thing? I'm sure you have.

Then there was another saying, "Successful people do those things that unsuccessful people fail to do." That may not be the exact quote, but you get the idea. And so did I. The message was clear. All I had to do was to look around and see what things I didn't want to do, realize that those were the things I would have to do, and then do them. Piece of cake. Nothing to it. So how come I wouldn't do them?

I know now that my imagination was limited to a "get-by" mentality. I had no awareness of the importance of creating a vision of who I might become. Instead I just kept playing the game of life by default—allowing my emotions to control me instead of vice-versa.

So how is your imagination? Is it creating a vision for success or a vision for failure. Are you doing those things you have to do to enable you to reach the success you would like? If not, ask yourself this question:

Is my dream for my future big enough to change the things I don't want to do into the things I will do—regardless?

Do not let who you were yesterday
determine who you will be tomorrow.

"How does one become a butterfly?"

"You must want to fly so much that you are Willing to give up being a caterpillar."

excerpt from
Hope for the Flowers
Trina Paulus

CHAPTER 8

The Quantum Leap

On January 1, 1957, I awakened with the biggest case of butterflies I had ever experienced. I felt like I was just about to participate in the Olympics and didn't even know what event I was entered in. I was scared to death.

What had I been thinking of when I decided to choose a new direction in my life? How could I have possibly thought I could sell as much life insurance in one year as I had during the previous four? What if I didn't make it? I must have been out of my mind. And, where in the world would I find the people to buy that much insurance? The butterflies never left me for the entire 365 days of my million dollar effort.

While the negative side of my thinking disparaged the idea that I could reach my goal, the fact is that I had burned so deeply into my brain and my heart the desire to change that nothing, absolutely nothing, was going to get in my way. Even so, I was continually plagued by fears. It is a wonder I didn't get ulcers.

My thinking reminds me of a question I was to hear later—"How do you eat an elephant?" The thought of what I had to do was so immense and overwhelming that I didn't know where to start.

The early part of January of my fifth year was the occasion for our company's regional meeting. At that meeting I passed the point of no return. I stood up in front of my peers, none of whom were million dollar producers (there were only two in our whole company) and announced my decision to the world. You would have thought that Bob Hope had just delivered a great one-liner. They really shouldn't have laughed, but I'm glad they did. They just added fuel to my fire.

By this time I had told all my friends what my plan was and while none of them laughed, I knew they were watching me. That in itself was a great motivator. So I began. I knew I couldn't keep using the city directory as my only source of prospects. I also knew that my reluctance to call on the people I knew had to come to a halt. From this moment on—EVERYONE became a prospect.

I started expanding my prospect list as quickly as I could. I called people I had previously sold (I could hardly call them clients yet), and offered to review their programs, and while they didn't exactly welcome me with open arms, I did get some appointments, and regardless of the outcome I started asking for referred leads.

Asking for a referred lead from a friend or policyholder was not a new idea. I just had never had the courage to consistently ask the question, "Who do you know?" But now those four words, along with an appropriate phrase such as—"who has just had a promotion or moved to town?" became a regular part of my vocabulary. I knew I had to tap every source I could imagine. It's amazing what happens when you go all out. I began to accumulate more prospects than I could call on. That meant I had to decide which ones were best and call on them first. My old way of thinking would have had me calling on the easiest ones first.

Planning became the next order of priority. I knew the results I wanted so now I had to get organized, even if I didn't really know what that meant. Here is where I would put Richard Campbell's "Friday Time" planning to the test. Little did I realize how hard that would be and the unbelievable results it would lead to.

Then I decided to take Frank Bettger's Weekly Time Table, and go one step further with it. I divided each day into 15 minute segments on the sheet. Instead of just deciding I wanted to contact a certain prospect sometime during the morning, I had to set a specific time to call or see him. I was apportioning my day.

I am convinced beyond question that the method I am about to describe to you, coupled with a non-negotiable mental contract with myself to reach a million dollars in life insurance sales in 1957, was the major ingredient for my success from this point on.

Here is exactly what I did:

Every Friday I selected the best 60 prospects from my 3" x 5" prospect card file. I then divided the 60 cards into two groups. One group I felt I must call on in person, and one group I felt could be contacted by telephone. I then took the "see" prospects (which included appointments already scheduled) and placed them in one of three stacks: Those who could be seen during the day, those who could be seen between 5:00 and 7:00 p.m. and those who could be seen between 7:00 and 10:00 o'clock in the evening. I then followed the same procedure with the "phone" group. When this was finished, the 60 prospects cards were in six groups.

The next step was the most difficult and time consuming part of my Friday planning. I had to take the "See" cards in the daytime category and transfer those names to the most appropriate spot on my weekly time table on Monday, Tuesday or Wednesday. Then I did the same for the 5-7 and the 7-10 "See" cards.

I followed exactly the same procedure for the "Phone" cards.

The net result of all this card sorting and transferring to the time control sheet was to have about 20 people to contact each day, either in person or by phone, on Monday, Tuesday, and Wednesday. Thursday morning was completely taken up by the detail work generated by the first 3 days work. Thursday afternoon was *Reward Time*— my time to play. Thursday night, like Monday, Tuesday and Wednesday nights was spent on phoning or having appointments.

Look at page 59 for one of my actual time sheets.

There was never a week that I managed to do everything on my time control sheet. However, I usually ended up completing at least 50% more contacts by Wednesday night using this plan than I had been able to accomplish in five or six days and four nights a week during my first four years.

In fact, look at a side-by-side summary comparison of effort and result between the months of January 1955, January, 1956 and January, 1957:

		Monday	Tuesday	Wednesday	Thursday	Friday
	8:00	Study	Study	Study		
	8:30	Study	Study	R & R Course		
M	9:00	Gene Bailey	Ray Schell	Wr. Jane		
O	9:15	Mel Brenneman	Clarence Robinson	Inf. for Huff		
R	9:30	Coburn Sr. Pol	John Niccum -61519	Earl Klinge		
N	9:45	Coburn sign form	Vern Nelson			
I	10:00	Albany Farm	Jack Weiss About Jim			
N	10:15	Rod Tripp	Bob Chase			
G	10:30	Rod Tripp	Bob Beall	Norma Dickson		
	10:45	Don Carmichael	Tom Jackson	Nita Gregory		
	11:00	Dwayne Johnson	Mel Beard	Curt Sorte		
	11:15	Jay Sorseth	Lv. for Corvallis	Bunt Jenks		
	11:30	Gene Bailey	Board Mtg. WVLU	Rea Cuniff 6 1265	Ame's Policies &	
	11:45	Curt Sorte	Board Mtg. WVLU	Bill Endicott	Thermometer	
	12:00	Sorseth	Ass'n Meeting	(Sorte)		
N	12:15	Policy to Hendricks				
O	12:30					
O	12:45					
N	1:00					
	1:15	Jerry Westbrook		Ralph Wade		
	1:30	Orin Wright				
	1:45	Vaughn Clausau	Badger Butler	Pat Shumway		
	2:00	Eldon Nass	LaVern Saboe			
A	2:15	Carolyn Rissman	Richard Marlatt			
F	2:30	Rita Mace	Lonnie Hallock			
T	2:45	Capt. Guitteriz	Smith Sig.			
E	3:00	Hi School	Nova's Box			
R	3:15	O'Brien Sig	Dick Reid			
N	3:30		Pens to Baroch			
O	3:45					
O	4:00	Peggy Webster				
N	4:15	Oz Williams				
	4:30	Bonnie VanHoosen	Policy to Dick Moore			
	4:45	Dick Hagerman				
	5:00	Dinner	Dinner	Dinner		
	5:15					
	5:30			Herb Giggs		
	5:45	Ron Lindsy	Hawk Policy Box	James Maxwell		
	6:00	Don Howard		Bob Barlow		
	6:15	Mark Mace	Lt. Roy Eury	Jim McCary		
	6:30	Craig Marble	Lt. Larry Biddison	Cal Dennis		
	6:45	Rudy Rojas	Lt. Loren Evanson	Charles Coffee		
E	7:00	Herb Chilstrom	Lt. Robt. MacDonald	Dave Bender		
V	7:15	Book Cook	Lt. Dan Thompson	Leland Fisher		
E	7:30	Jim Prochnau	Bob Hamilton	John Riley		
N	7:45	Loren Free	Carl Simon	Glen Dalson		
I	8:00	Nile Hoover	Dalton Cooley	Don Bailey		
N	8:15	Jim Plunkett	Dave Harmon	Ron Bryan		
G	8:30	Phil Zerr	Don Ridenour	Marshall Swink		
	8:45	Pat Kelly		Gale Scobee		
	9:00					

	<u>1955</u>	<u>1956</u>	<u>1957</u>
Total Hours	153	122	185
Total Calls	75	108	122
Closing Interviews	15	12	35
Sales	4	1	9
Volume	$9,500	$12,000	$119,500

There were other months in these three years that would have looked a little different, but I'm sure you get the idea. Having a big goal and directing great energy at it was going to make a difference.

Without tremendous enthusiasm, though, I doubt very much if I could have adequately planned my work or worked my plan. However, enthusiasm by itself was not enough. I was very enthusiastic early in my career with only mediocre results. I was to discover that time control depended on enthusiasm to create and carry out the plan, and that enthusiasm depended on time control to direct its energies. Time control became the president of my corporation and enthusiasm became my star salesman. Neither would have been able to function at their full potential without the other.

What an easy plan! On paper. It turned out that I never worked so hard in all my life. It took between six and eight hours of planning on Friday just to get ready for three blitz days.

Also note that I rewarded myself with Thursday afternoon off. However, my promise to myself that "Year of the Big Dream" was that if I had failed to schedule eight future interviews by Wednesday night, there would be no Thursday afternoon off. You saw by the record what the results were from the first month, but I will tell you right now that my goal of selling one million dollars of insurance was enhanced by the promise of Thursday afternoon off.

Because of the size of my goal, one other important area had to be improved if I was going to make it: More people would have to say yes to my presentation. I was going to have to become a better closer.

This went against my nature. I liked playing the nice guy and when a prospect said, "We'd like to think it over," my response had always been, "That's great. When would you like to have me check back with you?" You see, I was actually relieved to get some kind of decision, even if it was the wrong one. It meant I didn't have to face outright rejection.

But now things had to be different and the closing "technique" I am about to describe to you was the most difficult and most painful thing I had to do in my entire career.

Most of my prospects were husband and wife and I had learned to make my presentation in the living room with the three of us seated on the couch. I had learned by trial and error to have the wife sitting between me and the husband so that there was no chance for her to feel excluded—a practice that I stayed with during my entire career.

When I finished my presentation I asked the couple, "How does this sound to you?" Almost invariably they would look at each other then turn to me and say "We'd like to think it over." My reply was: "That is exactly what I don't want you to do."

What followed can only be described as a deadly silence. I could imagine the hairs on the back of their necks beginning to bristle. And I was so uncomfortable in that moment that I could hardly bear it.

Then I would say, "Let me tell you why I said that. I have kept excellent records over the past few years and I have discovered that out of every 21 people who have said to me what you just said, 19 have never bought insurance—from anyone. Now, if you're going to become a client of mine and if I am going to be the kind of insurance man you would like to have, I must find a way to help you get your program going. I'll be glad to step into the other room while you talk it over, but first let's take another look at what this program can do for you."

I made the statement with all the sincerity I owned. I really wanted them to make a decision because if they didn't they would go on for sometime in the future not owning the amount of insurance I thought they should.

I had been told that at the closing stage of the presentation someone was going to make a sale. Either the prospect was going to convince me that he didn't want to buy now, or I was going to convince him that the time was right. Up until 1957 the prospect was the best salesman.

But now I had a dream, and a little detour like, "We'd like to think it over," was not going to keep me from seeing it come true, even if I did have to endure that one moment of awful discomfort.

As I remember the intenseness of 1957, I often wonder what it is that comes into your life to make you completely change your way of looking at things. Is it the vision, the dream of things to come? That's obviously a major player in the game. But what is it that pushes you to dream in the first place? What is it that gives you a glimpse of who you might become?

I don't think it is just some kind of psychological phenomenon. I think it goes deeper than that. I once heard someone say that dreams are just God's way of telling us what is possible. I like that explanation.

Your logical brain is such a domineering brain that, without even realizing it, you allow it to put tremendous lids on your dreams. The, "I've never done anything yet to prove I'm special," type of mentality is rampant in almost all of us. We can't seem to fathom that there is a rough diamond deep inside each of us just waiting to be polished, so we use all kinds of excuses to keep from starting the process.

Reflections

I can remember in those first few years in the
insurance business when the task seemed so
enormous, and the amount of energy needed
seemed so vast, that I was almost too discouraged
to keep on trying. My five year promise kept
saving me. I would tell myself that if I wanted a
tree (my success) to grow I was going to have to
start by planting a seed. Then my limiting mind
would answer, "Yeah, but look how long it takes a
tree to grow. What if you don't last long enough to
reap the harvest?" The antics I would go through to
keep from moving ahead.

Even today, after all these years, I still find
myself with doubts. But I have developed another
fear that is stronger than my doubts. And it is much
stronger than the fear of failing. I have developed a
fear of failing to try. I have come to a point in my
life where I realize that the only way to fail in life
is to not try.

So anytime you began to doubt yourself, just
ask, "What if I don't go for it? How will I feel?"
My answers to those two questions come back to
me in the form of more questions: "If you don't try
Bill, will you be experiencing life at its best? Will
you be tapping your God-given talent, whatever it
is? Will you be living life with gusto?" I guess you

know my answers.

So how about you? The next time you hesitate, or you think the task sounds too difficult, or the prospect too tough, how about asking yourself some similar questions. If you don't get the right answers, you'd better think long and hard before handing over control of your life to your logical brain.

You know something else? You may be a youngster now compared to me, but every day you live gives you one less day to make it happen.

Just something to think about.

Do not compare yourself to anyone—
except the you that you can be.

"*Concerning all acts of initiative and
        creation,
There is one elementary truth—
That the moment one definitely commits
        oneself,
Then Providence moves too.*"

Goethe

CHAPTER 9

A Vision
Come True

I'm sure you've heard the phrase "The harder I work, the luckier I get." I had heard it too, but I had absolutely no idea what it was all about. For all I knew it was just some catchy phrase that someone made up.

For the first time in my adult life I was startled to learn that there are things that happen which seem kind of mystical. When you are pushing hard towards a definite goal, things happen that multiply your success, enhance your confidence, and build your self-esteem. It seemed as though some inexplicable force had come into my life when I demonstrated I was deadly serious about accomplishing my goal. Remember Thoreau's words from a previous chapter?

"If one advances confidently in the direction
of his dreams..."

But it went even deeper than this. I couldn't believe the seemingly coincidental things that happened. Without planning, I would be at the right place at the right time to meet a new prospect or renew acquaintances with a prospect I had called on before without success. Many times I had friends come up to me at a social gathering or during a golf game and ask me if I had called on so and so who had just moved into town, or they made me aware of a career promotion or other positive change happening to someone they knew. They seemed to know I was serious about my goal and wanted to help.

I also discovered a secret that I have lived by ever since. I was so charged with my dream and the gargantuan effort I was making to have it come true that my energy level must have been percolating off the charts. The result was that when anyone asked, "How are you doing?" my automatic response was, "Really Great!!!" Without my realizing it, my tremendously positive attitude was going to affect my entire future. What happened was that the word began to spread around Albany that I was doing well.

It's amazing how much information gets traded around during coffee breaks. Word of mouth began to make me a success before the fact and had a positive effect on me. It was not long before it was commonplace for someone to see me and mention that he or she had heard that I was doing well. Of course, I enthusiastically answered in the affirmative. "Really Great!" became my battle cry. The more I answered that way, the more people told me they'd heard about my success. The more I heard that the more I believed it myself. What a great feeling it was to have people pat me on the back and say, "Glad to hear you're doing so good." "Really Great" changed the way people looked at me, and changed the way I looked at myself.

At that time in my life, science had not yet discovered the importance of positive self-talk and the role it plays in success or failure. And I wasn't to discover what I was doing right until years later. But the fact was that I was programming myself for success by the words I was saying and the picture of success I was holding in my mind. I was setting up other forces to come into play to help me on the way.

The first part of 1957 was one of frenzied activity. I was running off in every direction trying anything and everything to get appointments. I tried different telephone approaches. I was constantly aware of who I was seeing around town and whether or not they were people I could get to meet on a favorable basis. And this frenzy was working, but I still had no track to run on. Then another "coincidence" came into my life by the name of Ken Ray. Ken was a leading premium producer for Western Life and I knew I was going to see him at a convention in Sun Valley in June (I had barely qualified with my minimum production in 1956). I called Ken and asked if he could give me some of his time at the convention to see if he could help me with some ideas on reaching my goal. He agreed, we met, and my life changed again.

Ken kept his method of operation very simple. He called only on people in the armed forces, and presented one idea. He used a prepared sales talk, called "The Success Plan." It was a presentation on how to save money, through a life insurance policy, to supplement government retirement. The one small army base near our town, Camp Adair was staffed with just a few service people, but the idea of helping them build a nest egg for their retirement really appealed to me. I decided to adopt Ken's sales talk, verbatim, and give it to everyone I could, including civilians.

We visited Gloria's folks on the way back home from the convention. I used the whole week there to memorize the sales talk. It was only 20 minutes in length, but as I was to find out that takes some powerful concentrating. But my goal was still burning and when we got back home I was ready. Every approach and every interview for the rest of the year was made around "The Success Plan." I became so charged about the importance of people saving money that my closing ratio began to improve and my dream of one million dollars in sales was coming closer to reality.

I had become a million dollar producer the moment I irrevocably created a vision in my mind of who I believed I could be, as I watched Bob Cummins drive away in his expensive car. I wanted his lifestyle to be mine. Now I was merely turning my vision into reality.

I began to write more polices and bigger policies (that really meant more $12,000 policies and less $5,000 policies). I began to schedule a few daytime appointments, something that had seemed almost impossible a year earlier. I began to call on people who made more money than I. (Which was just about everyone). I became more confident in my approach and much more dedicated to making the sale if I felt the solution was right—and in my mind everyone needed to save money.

And talk about calling on friends. I had to do a little talking to myself about my goal and finally I even called on my folks. They couldn't say no to listening, but my step-dad, Eveard Fish, a wonderful man, asked me more questions than I had ever heard. Each time I had to reply "I don't know, but I can find out." After about four interviews

I finally made the sale, a $10,000 Retirement Income policy (The Success Plan). It was the hardest sale I made that year, but also the best sale since now I had the answers I needed. Never again with the Success Plan did I have to say "I don't know."

There is an interesting side note on that sale. Eveard was about age 45 when I sold him the policy—the only policy he ever bought—and it promised to give him $22,000 at age 62. When he reached age 62, my mother and he took the money and put it into a certificate of deposit. Eveard is now 80 years old, and that $22,000 has grown to over $100,000. Having to find the answers those tough questions turned out to be good for everyone.

Remember when I wrote that one of my beliefs was that no one would buy insurance in December? Well in 1957 they had no choice. Nor did I have time to work in the clothing store because I still had a ways to go to reach my goal. Finally, just before Christmas, the magic day happened. I topped a million in sales. I only had to get the last policy issued and my dream would come true. On December 31, 1957 my final record of new insurance produced stood at $1,000,014. I've got to admit I had to increase my own insurance program by $50,000, to keep up with my new vision of success, as part of that total. But it was kind of like graduating from college. No one asks you about your grades—only whether you graduated. And did I graduate. I was a Million Dollar Producer.

It is impossible for me to describe in words the feeling that came over me when I reached my goal. I can only say that it stands out in my memory right along with the night I was awarded my Eagle Scout badge. A tremendous feeling of accomplishment and satisfaction.

The only problem, as I was to realize, was that once

you've reached a goal, you can't go back. Oh sure, I could
have been a flash in the pan—a one time performer—and
then sunk back into obscurity. But the feeling of real
accomplishment was too great not to want to experience it
again. I swore I would never go back. Besides I was riding
a big wave. So why not set my sights higher? I could whip
the world.

I can't believe what I did next. I actually stood up
in front of the same peer group at our January 1958
regional meeting and announced:

"This year I am going to produce $2,000,000 of
insurance."

I wished they had laughed. They didn't. They
cheered. Why did I have to open my big mouth? No one in
our entire company had ever written two million in one
year. I must have been temporarily insane. A miracle
would have to happen. I could feel the butterflies in my
stomach reassembling for action.

Reflections

*E*very once in a while I look back at that pivotal month of October, 1956 and wonder what my life would have been like if I hadn't decided to take the biggest risk of my career up to that point.

No doubt I would have gone on to some other career—selling clothing or cars or washers and dryers, or climbing the ladder of the corporate world, probably still in sales since I seemed oriented toward people.

I believe that eventually I would have ended up selling real estate or stocks and bonds, as friends of mine have grown wealthy doing. All I can say now however, looking back at 1957 and that $1,000,014 of sales, is that I'm glad it was insurance and that I was given the opportunity to experience all the wonderful years that followed.

There will come moments in your life when you'll get the chance to decide to go for it. All it takes is for you to say "yes" to one of those opportunities, and, like mine, your life will be changed forever.

So my wish for you is that when opportunity and risk come knocking, you will open the door and say with eagerness and enthusiasm, "Step right in!"

You never reach your potential
the farther you go, the farther you can see.

"What you can do,
Or dream you can do, begin it;
Boldness has genius, power and magic in it."

Goethe

CHAPTER 10

Raising
My Sights

So what had changed to take me from dismal failure to flying high in one year? The decision to become a million dollar producer had elevated my thinking from survival to visions of success.

But now, to write $2,000,000 of insurance in 1958 the way I operated in 1957 seemed impossible. I felt that I was working at maximum effort. There is a trap which almost all sales people seem to fall into at one time or another in their careers which is stated this way:

*If what you're doing is working successfully,
stop doing it and start doing something else.*

However, there is another maxim that has worked well for me several times and it is this:

There is nothing wrong with fixing that which is

not broken, if by doing so it is taken to a higher
level of performance.

In my case the abandonment of my old system, instead of leading to disaster as it might have, led me to the discovery of an idea that was to change my thinking and my way of selling forever.

One of Northwestern Mutual Life's all-time great general agents is a man named Al Granum. He is a legend in the insurance profession, and is noted for his dynamic leadership as well as for creating the now well-known and widely used "One Card System," a detailed method for operating a successful life insurance practice. I don't believe the "One Card System" was in existence yet, but another Al Granum idea caught my attention. It was a very simple method of determining the insurance needs of a prospect.

It was about this same time that Prudential Insurance Co. was encouraging its agents to use what was called "The Planned Dollar Guide," a multi-colored bar chart that demonstrated to a prospect exactly what Social Security benefits would be paid in the case of his death, plus what his present assets, combined with existing and proposed insurance, would leave in an estate for his family. All very orderly and colorful. The problem was that somebody forgot to train the prospects in chart reading. They quickly forgot how to interpret them. When I called on these same prospects, they would ask me to explain the charts but I couldn't read them either. I had an aversion to any chart or graph. I didn't even like reading the instructions for assembling a child's toy at Christmas. My own Friday planning used all the energy reserve I had for details. I needed a plan to show prospects that was simple enough for an Irishman like me to understand without having to study it.

Al Granum saved me. His program did the same thing as the Prudential plan, but instead of a chart, he used simple English language to show Mr. and Mrs. Prospect a plan for reaching their objectives. It was a four-page proposal that simply showed:

Page 1	A- Family members and ages
	B- Present life insurance owned
Page 2	Objectives in the event of death or retirement
Page 3	A- What present insurance, social security and assets would do towards accomplishing the desired objectives
	B- Insurance amount needed to cover any shortage
Page 4	Summary page showing objectives accomplished after new insurance added

To the above presentation I added my "Purple Sheet," the proposal I had used with the "Success Plan." It was a simple two page summary showing the value of the suggested new insurance at the 10th and 20th year, and at age 65.

This simple plan was to become my M.O., my method of operation, for the rest of my career. Over time the type of prospects I called on changed, but the simplicity stayed the same—except for a period of "Complicated Sophistication" which I will talk about later.

I adopted Al Granum's method part and parcel, put an attractive blue binder around it and picked up the tempo on my $2,000,000 goal.

But the new plan was important for another reason that was to shape my entire future. Most life insurance salespeople of this era were selling package plans, "I've got a great idea I would like to show you." I believe it was New York Life that started what would become an industry standard with a "You'll Earn a Fortune" presentation on saving money just like my "Success Plan". (I think my company took New York Life's idea and just changed the name).

At any rate, small package sales, whether they encouraged the prospect to save money or to buy a $10,000 policy for protection, were the norm for the day. My entire future was to change because of the concept of establishing needs and offering solutions. The need might be to save money, and the solution might be a "Success Plan," but never again would I offer a solution that wasn't based on a need identified by the client instead of a solution I had pre-decided upon. And the prospects who became clients appreciated the process. They liked knowing exactly what their estate, no matter how small, would look like in the event of premature death. And they especially enjoyed the idea that when they reached retirement age, their income would be greatly enhanced. When I made that decision to go from package presentor to problem solver, I stepped from salesman to professional and added a whole new meaning to my daily efforts.

Solving a need for my client was a lot more fun for me, and immeasurably more satisfying for everyone involved. It was like playing detective. I located the prospect's problem and solved it. Definitely a "Win-Win" situation. As it turned out, "Needs Basis" selling became far more profitable over the years than the package sale approach I had used before.

As the end of 1958 came in sight I was on a roll. Then it happened. I came down with what was called the "hard flu." It was the kind that kept you in bed for 10 days and left you drained (I now wonder if this was some kind of subconscious reaction to the pressure I had put myself under). It was about the 5th of December, and I didn't get out of bed until the 15th. Guess what happened? My pre-million dollar production thinking came back into play. How could I possibly write any more insurance between December 15 and December 31. Who would want to buy at this time of year?

Why did I start this limiting thinking? I believe there was one major reason:

My goal to write $2,000,000 was a goal based on what I WANTED to do—rather than what I HAD TO DO.

I had not put myself under the pressure of, "I must—with no excuses." Also the question of my own self-worth was not quite as strong a driving force as the year before. Even if I quit on the 15th, I could still be proud of what I had accomplished. And so I decided to spend the next two weeks getting my strength back and getting ready for Christmas and the New Year. In retrospect, I'm not pleased with myself for giving up, but at least I didn't go back to work in the clothing store. I was now committed to my profession—and to a little time off.

I ended up 1958 with a production record of $1,759,500. That was more than seven times as much as I had done two years earlier, and in today's dollars represented a sales achievement in excess of $8,000,000. What a tremendous feeling even for falling short of my

goal. As I used to say, if I was going to fail to reach my
goal, I couldn't think of a nicer way to do it.

Just to give you an idea of how much a change in
attitude can make, here is a side-by-side comparison of an
average 1956 and 1958 week and month (I calculated these
results based upon ten months of actual work effort, so as
not to reflect time spent on meetings, conventions, and
vacations).

Effort	1956	%incr	1958
Calls-wk	21	50%	32
Interviews-wk	4	50%	6
Hours-wk	32	30%	42
Results			
sales-mo	4	150%	10
volume-mo	$21,550	800%	$175,950
each call	$3.14	234%	$8.15
closing ratio	1-4+	100%	1-2+
Ea. Interview	$16.80	260%	$43.63

*Moral: You do not have to double your effort
to double your results!*

The long reaching results of these two years of
supreme effort would bring more to my family and me than
I could ever have realized at this time. My dreams were
about to come true—over and over and over again.

And, by the way, thank you Alfred O. Granum,
CLU. I owe you one. Big time.

Reflections

I recently saw figures that established a law of averages. They were based on Al Granum's One Card System and reflected, recorded and documented agent activity for a total of 25 years with a major analysis at the 15th, 20th, and 25th years. The study dealt with 100,000 prospects, 30,000 fact-finding interviews, and 10,000 eventual sales. This established a 10-3-1 ratio which I call a "law for the masses."

Any new agent with the desire to produce can prove these figures over a period of time. They are the standard for the industry. What they are not is a standard for any one individual. In other words, a 10-3-1 ratio of calls to fact-finding interviews to eventual sales sets the standard for the average results an agent should expect.

What neither you nor I know is what your results will be. What else we don't know is what your results could be. What they are and what they could be are almost always two different factors.

If you've been in selling for any length of time you know exactly how many prospects you have to ask to buy to obtain one sale. If you're like most of us you have a tendency to set your annual production goal around the knowledge of how many people you will have to see and ask to buy to make your new goal.

I propose that thinking like that limits you and your future. What if, by some feat of magic, I could come to you and wipe out the knowledge that your closing ratio is one out of three and replace it with the absolute knowledge that your personal closing ratio is one out of two. And because that is your truth, you went out and performed to your expectations.

"Yeah, but I know that I'm a 1-out-of-3 closer," you say. "I've proved it over the past five years." If you're stubborn enough, you will stay with that judgement and my magic will lose. But if you are open to a new idea, then here it is:

A big dream just might improve your closing ratio.

Will you agree with me that you don't even know for sure what your potential really is? If you agree, then let me suggest to you that your potential for closing sales is unlimited. Putting it another way, it is limited, but only as you make it so.

Logic, however, will not change your closing ratio. Better closing skills will change it only a little bit. The only thing that will change it forever is a dream so big that nothing will stop you from achieving it. A dream that excites you and moves you to action. A dream that fills you with enthusiasm and energy. And when you have a dream that big, you will discover that you have a vision of who and what you can be.

So let me wish for you the discovery of what it is that will make you move mountains. And who knows, you just might enjoy being a mountain mover.

Records are made to be broken—
and mountains are there to be moved.

*"Perspective is a road sign
Showing how far you have come.
Wisdom is recognizing how far
You have yet to go."*

William L. O'Hearn
Famous Irish Philosopher

CHAPTER 11

Lost Perspective

In 1959, with the reestablished goal of $2,000,000 in sales I started moving faster and faster. For the previous seven years all I really had to do was to sell, but now my commitment to solving the insurance problems of my clients and servicing them on an annual basis was beginning to put additional demands on my time. However, I had learned somewhere that the average person buys life insurance seven times in his life, and I was determined to be there on each occasion. As suggested by Al Granum, I was committed to an annual review whether it was time to add coverage or not.

The good news was that it was really enjoyable visiting with old clients and friends. More good news was that there was no call reluctance on my part in reaching for the telephone to set up program review appointments. The bad news was that it was easy to convince myself that I was working effectively. After all, a call on a client counted the same in my record book as a call on a new prospect. At least that was my rationale.

The One Card System was to eventually address this problem, but in the meantime I was left to the only thing I understood. Work harder—but not smarter.

The problem was that I had never liked hard work. Oh, I would do it if I was working towards an exciting goal, but just to keep turning the grindstone for the sake of earning money or even for the sake of turning the grindstone, as I had observed other people doing, would not cut it for me.

I was between a rock and a hard place. What could I possibly do to force myself to keep pushing? I decided I needed a reward. I decided that in exchange for going for the 16 percent increase in sales which would give me the numbers to exceed $2,000,000, Gloria and I would treat ourselves to a trip to Hawaii for a three-week vacation in June of 1960. We hadn't been able to afford a one-week vacation on our own, but thanks to company conventions we were enjoying one each year. Sure, I was now a "Big Producer," but I was just getting out of debt from the first four years. Besides, I was also raising our standard of living, and it didn't seem like there was much more money than before. Little did I realize that this was to be an ongoing phenomenon.

The real frosting on the cake though, the real incentive, would be the fulfillment of a dream I had held for years. While we were in Hawaii I would attend my first Million Dollar Round Table meeting. I would get to meet the big hitters and at the same time see how they were solving the problem of too much to do and too little time to do it. This incentive was all I needed. Watch out world, I was going for it again.

I thought I had found the answer to incentive-related action. And I had. Temporarily.

And so it began. Running harder and faster. Harder and faster. I still stuck to the discipline of my ideal work week. Friday, all day for planning. Monday, Tuesday and Wednesday running from early morning to late at night. Keep up with my CLU studies. Thursday morning for details, Thursday afternoon off to take a deep breath and back at it Thursday night. Something was wrong in my life, but I was too focused to comprehend what it was.

Then another significant "coincidence" happened. Grant Taggart from Cowley, Wyoming, was coming to town to speak at the Portland Life Underwriters Annual Sales Congress, an event that would attract 600-700 producers from all over the state. Grant was a legend in the life insurance industry, and I couldn't wait to hear him.

When the big day came, I had made the decision to try to get his attention for just a moment after he spoke, and ask him just one question. It was:

"How much is enough?"

I was going to ask this great man to help me solve the dilemma the question posed. I realized that I was frightened of a future that held out the grim prospect of cumulative years of one sales record after another. Would I go on into infinity just grinding out numbers? And what happened if I couldn't do it? Would I be less of a man? Would I be a failure after all? When could I stop lifting the cross on my back? When could I say it was okay, and that I was okay, regardless of increased production? How much is enough?

The big day finally arrived, and Grant Taggart was

all I hoped he would be. What a beautiful, kind person. You could see why he was a success. People liked being around him. I don't remember how old he was at the time, but he seemed definitely old enough to be a grandfather figure.

There was a break in the meeting after his talk and people were crowded around him trying to shake his hand. When my turn finally came, I looked him in the eye and said I needed to ask him a very important question. With just a bit of explanation I then asked, "How much is enough?" He answered, "Why don't you just wait around a bit until I'm finished here, and we'll go have a cup of coffee."

I couldn't believe it. This great man was going to spend some time with me. I was to find out later that this was the norm with MDRT members, but right then I couldn't believe it.

I started the conversation by relating in short form my rise from "failure to success," and Grant gave me his full attention. When I had finished he said, "Let me tell you a story." I cannot remember his exact words, but here is the gist of what he said:

There was a young man who had a very successful father. After finishing college, the young man went on to dental school, started a dental practice and unbeknownst to his father made a decision to become not only the best dentist in town, but more successful than his dad.

As his practice grew he began to work harder and harder, starting earlier and ending later. He must have been thinking that if he could make a lot of money fast that he would be proving himself. He was putting so much pressure on himself that he began to drink. Not too much at first, but gradually more and more. The harder he worked, the more he drank, and the more he drank the more he neglected the fine family he had started. He didn't have time for his children and his wife was at her wit's end. He wouldn't listen to anyone and he wouldn't slow down. To keep himself on his tremendously demanding schedule he began to take drugs—just to keep going.

His friends began to avoid him, and finally his wife left him, taking the children with her. In her eyes a machine had replaced her husband and the children's father. He had actually become possessed with the need to succeed.

Grant stopped for a minute, looked me right in the eye and said quietly, hesitating for a moment, "And last week we buried my son."

I was absolutely stunned. Tears came to my eyes, as they have every time I've ever told this story. I couldn't speak. I didn't know what to say. Here was this great man, a week after his son's funeral, keeping his commitment to his profession and taking time to help a stranger. His grief must have been immense. He was faced with the thought that his own success, which he had kept in perspective, had somehow influenced his son to lose his.

I could only imagine Grant's thoughts. From my perspective, I felt that anyone would have been blessed to have Grant Taggart as a father. So why had his son lost perspective?

Over the next several days I pondered how anyone could be so driven as to lose sight of the importance of life. And the more I thought, the clearer Grant's message became:

*No amount of success is worth sacrificing
your family, your friends or your life.*

This rule was to eventually shape my philosophy
and, as I matured, the following became my adage:

There is no success in numbers.

Then, however, all I could do was to make a vow to
myself that I would keep my insurance production goal in
line and in balance with the rest of my life. I knew that I
would never go back to being less than a million dollar
producer, but I was determined not to live my life chained
to selling bigger and bigger amounts of life insurance.

Grant died in 1979, but his lesson has never left me.
Thank you, Grant, for taking the time to touch the life of a
stranger—forever!

Reflections

*A*s I look back over the years, I realize I didn't always remember Grant Taggart's lesson. There were times when I would get out of balance. Yet as I gained more and more experience, I gained more perspective and eventually was able to set my ego aside and stop tying my self-worth to production.

This was difficult to do because I had identified myself with what I did more than who I was. Since the great majority of my everyday activity was taken up with being an insurance man, the majority of my thinking was how to be a better insurance man. Being better, too much of the time, meant being bigger. It would be a while before I realized that bigger has *nothing* to do with better. All of us have seen people at the top of their profession who lacked the qualities we would associate with great human beings.

Just a few years ago, a very wise man put this all into perspective for me. He said, "Bill, God doesn't care what you do. He only cares who you are." Then he went on to give me some advice that I work hard to follow. I would like to pass his thoughts on to you. He said to me,

> *"Bill, the only thing you have to be aware of, whether you are selling insurance, talking to a friend, or being with*

your family, is the quality of your presence. No matter what you are doing, strive at each moment to be the very best you can be."

As I look back now, I can see that in my pursuit of being the best insurance sales professional I could be, I sometimes forgot to pursue being the best husband, father, friend or human being I could be.

Maybe you might like to take a little time and consider the depth of my friend's statement as it applies to your own life. Are you striving at each moment to be the best you can be? Or are you striving in only one or two areas and letting some of the rest slide?

From moment to moment, which is what your life is all about, would it be worthwhile to stay aware of *the quality of your presence?*

Just something to think about.

Big numbers might not bring you long term happiness, but long term happiness might bring you big numbers.

"Try not to become a man of success
But rather try to become a man of value."

Albert Einstein

CHAPTER 12

Gained
Perspective

Resolving to never lose perspective about what success was all about, and doing something about it were two different things. I could convince myself to stay at my current level of production and not drive for more and more, but also I did not want to go backwards. That meant I had to keep my present level of commitment to my profession. That part was okay. Somehow, though, I had to find more time for the other areas of my life.

Gloria and I now had three daughters, Molly, Patti and Julie, all born within a two and one-half year period. I wanted to spend more time with them and with Gloria.

My first decision after talking with Grant Taggart may have seemed illogical if I had explained it to anybody. I decided that if I was to add quality to my life I would need a little more time for me. My decision was easy. I would take off all day Thursdays instead of just Thursday afternoon. This meant I would have to become even more efficient with the management of the details of my insurance business. But I was optimistic because I had discovered a truth that seemed universal:

If the goal is inspiring enough, you can find a way to make it happen.

Hawaii and the Million Dollar Round Table fulfilled that maxim for me. There was no way I was not going to be in Hawaii in June.

I didn't really do things much differently than before, but I did have to allocate time more effectively. As a result, an interesting thing happened. By taking all day Thursday to play, or work in the yard, or do just whatever I wanted, I became energized. My spirit was renewed. I came back on Friday ready to fight a grizzly bear. I was charged with a "let's-get-at-it" attitude. And that attitude carried through the weekend, so when Monday morning came around I was ready to tackle anything for the next three days—and nights—knowing of course that another *Thursday* was coming.

There was an interesting paradox occuring about this time. In our area there were six agents who represented The Prudential Insurance Company, one of the most respected companies in America. One of the things Prudential did better than anyone else was to train its agents in the science of selling life insurance. As part of that program every Prudential agent in our area was required to drive to the agency office in Salem, and spend each Friday morning in training and planning the next week. While The Prudential, like most other companies with an agency system, was teaching its agents the nuts and bolts of the life insurance business, in my mind it was failing to impart more than just the science of selling. And a belief that I have maintained from that time to this is:

All the training in the world cannot create a great sales person. The science of "how" imparts only knowledge. If the talent of a sales person is to be tapped there must first be an established motive, created by the agent—not the manager. A motive strong enough to give the agent inspiration when the going gets tough. In other words, there must be a "why" on top of the "how." Without a "why," no one will ever reach for the stars.

The proof of this statement was reflected in the 1959 production of those six Prudential agents. These were men with talent. They had excellent training according to the insurance industry norm. I was no better than they were, nor were they any more talented than I was. Yet when the final figures were in, my sales—for one reason only—exceeded the total combined sales of these six agents. This was not a reflection on their ability. Only on their lack of training in the critical area of visionary goal setting. What made me run had more energy behind it than what made them run. And I understood that. I had spent four years learning nuts and bolts and operating with survival as a goal. *In the end, the only difference between me and them, was the size of my inspiration.*

Reflections

*D*uring this period of my life, I was not aware of Parkinson's law which states that human beings have a tendency to expand the job to fit the time available. This means that if you have a four-day job and five days to get it done, you will probably spread the job over five days.

But I believe the reverse is also true. If you have a five-day job and you need to get it done in four, you will usually get it done in four.

Have you asked yourself lately if you are you doing the best job possible in the shortest time available, or, if are you expanding the job to fit the time? If the latter is true, I suggest there is a possibility that you do not have business and avocation goals big enough to excite you.

There is a great opportunity to gain balance in your life by establishing a meaningful goal, defining the effort needed, expending it in the shortest time possible, and then spending the freed-up time with your family or in the pursuit of a fulfilling hobby.

You will find that your mind becomes more creative. You have more energy. Your enthusiasm grows by leaps and bounds, and you discover new meaning to your life.

It happened to me. I know it can happen to you. Give it a try. You'll be amazed at the results.

With a strong enough why,
you can endure any how.

"Change your thoughts
And you change your world."

Norman Vincent Peale

CHAPTER 13

A Myth
Bites The Dust

The trip to Hawaii in 1959 was a fantastic experience for Gloria and me. We did not take the children with us. It was our vacation, and our reward for paying the price for success—and it was our success because there was absolutely no way I could have kept up the pace without Gloria's encouragement, support, and management of our home.

The Round Table meeting was held at Kaiser's Hawaiian Village on Waikiki Beach on Oahu. The meeting was truly unbelievable. I was amazed that there could be so many million dollar producers under one roof, all willing and eager to share information. I was awestruck.

One of the main platform speakers who impressed me greatly was a young man named Larry Wilson. He had entered the insurance business at age 23 and at age 29 became the youngest Lifetime Member of the Million Dollar Round Table. The title of his presentation in Hawaii was "How I developed a pension business from scratch to 100 cases in four years." Here I was, three years older than Larry and I couldn't even spell pension. And I sure didn't know anyone who would buy something as complicated as a pension plan from someone as young as we were.

What did Larry have that I didn't have? I'll bet anything he had a bigger dream. Larry left the insurance business shortly after that and formed Wilson Learning Corporation which most of you have heard about. He went on to create *Counselor Selling* which is still having a huge impact on the entire selling profession. Larry also co-authored the book, *The One Minute Sales Person* with Spencer Johnson, and in 1987 authored the very popular book, *Changing the Game*. He is now chairman and CEO of *Pecos River Learning Centers Inc.* in Santa Fe. Larry has had an tremendous career. I'll bet it was influenced positively by those early years in the insurance business.

Another man in Hawaii entered my life for a few minutes and gave me insight into just how limiting my thinking had been—and still was at that time.

I met Nate Kaufman on the beach at Waikiki. I recognized him because one of the industry's magazines published an All-Star roster annually. One person from each company was selected by his company as All-Star of the Year and his picture was put in the magazine. I used to go through the magazine and read the information under each photo. Nate had been the All-Star more times for his company than anyone else from any other company. I remember reading "All Star - 22 consecutive years" after Nate's name. This man was in a league by himself, and yet he was willing to spend some time with me to share a couple of thoughts.

The first thing he told me was that he had decided

years before that Christmas would be a great time for grandparents to buy a life insurance policy as a gift for their grandchildren. Nate explained that as a result of that kind of thinking, the previous December had marked the eighth year in a row in which he had sold one million dollars of insurance—in December. This put to rest the myth I had held earlier in my career that *no one buys insurance in December.* This man would sell as much insurance in one month as most successful agents sold in a year.

Then he shared another idea with me. One that I never put into action but still believe to this day would have raised me to further heights had I tried it. Nate told me that every year he would have a party for his best clicnts and included anyone who had bought from him that ycar for the first time. He rented the Elks lodge and hosted a party for about 200 of his clients. Not only did his clients appreciate being asked, they also enjoyed meeting others to whom Nate had sold insurance. He said that while making new sales was definitely not the purpose of the party, new sales always resulted—especially in the grandparent/ grandchild market.

A Million Dollars every December! What ever made me think I was working to capacity?

What did I take away from that meeting with Nate? For the first time in my life I began to realize that hard work by itself just wouldn't accomplish all the things I wanted to experience in my life. I was going to have to find a way to work smarter. Did that mean I was going to find it difficult to work smarter? Probably.

Reflections

$\mathcal{A}$s I reflect now on what I thought *working smarter* meant to me, I realize that I thought I actually had to get a lot smarter. To me that meant spending more time on my CLU studies, more time learning about business and estate planning, and more time acquiring product knowledge. What I didn't realize was that *working smarter* was supposed to mean becoming *more effective*.

Many times over the years I became very efficient and confused it with effectiveness. Sporadically, I would keep my desk neat and uncluttered. I admired and tried to emulate friends who had a place for everything and everything in its place. What never occurred to me was that I had to have a reason to do better. Just wanting to because I thought it would be nice had no power in it. Somehow I confused efficiency and effectiveness.

Many of the time management plans that are on the market today will help you be efficient, but a time management plan is only as effective as the goal of the user. In other words, unless you are really focused on an end result—a goal, you might end up checking everything off your list at the end of the day and find you really didn't move forward.

So let me urge you to keep raising your sights about what you want to accomplish. *Find your reason to succeed* and you will find yourself becoming more effective. And that's working smarter.

Set yearly goals between Christmas and New Year's.

Update those goals over the Fourth of July weekend.

"Desire is the key to motivation, but it's the determination and commitment to an unrelenting pursuit of your goal—a commitment to excellence—that will enable you to attain the success you seek."

Mario Andretti

CHAPTER 14

Learning From The Leaders

The lessons I had learned at the Million Dollar Round Table meeting in Hawaii in 1960 influenced me greatly and at future Round Table meetings I was to meet several more leaders who would raise my sights and give me new perspective.

The 1966 MDRT meeting was held in Boston and on the first day, at lunch, I was introduced to a young man named Joe Gandolfo. I had not heard his name before but from the talk that was going around he would soon be known.

Joe was twenty-five years old and had been in the business for about three or four years. In 1965 he had sold 410 cases for a total of $5,100,000 of volume. This was an unbelievable work effort and made the rest of us look like we were standing still. I had to learn more about what he was doing.

As good luck would have it, Joe loved to play

handball, as did I, so we scheduled a game at the YMCA. We played a couple of local players and won. From that point on Joe always introduced me as "My doubles partner—we've never been beaten." We were given the chance to prove that, not always successfully, over the next few years, but important to this chapter is our getting together the next year in Lucerne, Switzerland for the 1967 MDRT meeting.

All the annual meetings are special, but this one was exceptionally so. With Frank Sullivan as the 1967 MDRT president, and presentations by the great John Todd, who urged us to accept that, "There are no Ceilings," and Viktor Frankl who shared his experiences in a concentration camp, and his book, *Man's Search for Meaning,* which the Round Table had given to all of us attending, it was an outstanding meeting.

While we were in Lucerne, Gloria and I took Joe and his wife Carol out to dinner in order for the four of us to get acquainted. It was a fun evening and we decided to meet after the Round Table meeting for some sightseeing in Rome.

After a few days in Rome, Joe and Carol left for Nice, France and Gloria and I headed for Florence. We agreed to meet in Nice a week later for another evening out before flying to Paris.

A week later, Gloria and I were having so much fun shopping that we got a late start for our dinner date 240 kilometers away. Since it was approximately 144 miles from Florence to Nice, I figured to drive it in about three hours, so I called Joe and said we would meet them for a late, after dinner, dessert.

We left Florence at 7 o'clock in the evening and at ten o'clock I called Joe again and said we would just have to meet them at the airport in the morning.

After driving up and down one mountain after another for twelve hours we finally arrived at the Nice airport just in time to catch our flight. So much for my Grand Prix driving talent.

And now to the point of the story—my next learning experience in what is possible.

Gloria and Carol decided to sit together on the flight to Paris which gave Joe and me the opportunity for some one-on-one conversation. And it went like this:

Joe: "How many closing interviews did you have last year (1966)?"

My answer, as I remember, reflected a decent work effort and what I thought was a great closing ratio—something better than one sale for every two interviews. I do remember exactly, however, what Joe's reply was to my query about his 1966 effort. In that year he had 385 closing interviews and 583 sales. Naturally I asked how that was possible. Joe said that when he completed a sale to the head of the household, he automatically saw to it that the spouse and children got some coverage too, and since he was already at their house he did not count it as another interview. There went my conception or rather misconception of how many interviews it took to get a sale. Everyone else I knew, including myself, would have counted every little interview just so they could convince themselves they were really working.

Joe and I stayed friends over the years and I followed his career with great interest. I gathered these facts about Joe's production the next few years after Lucerne:

1968 - Total Sales Volume - $22,000,000
1969 - Total Sales Volume - $32,000,000
1970 - Total Sales Volume - $73,000,000 (on 810 lives
                              with $776,000 in premium)

Joe was in a league by himself, but his records did let the rest of us know that there was no lid on what we could accomplish should we decide to pay the price that he had paid.

The Million Dollar Round Table was a performance measuring vehicle for me, and was responsible for adding many dimensions to my thinking over the next several years. Making friends with such men as Tom Wolff made my path in the insurance profession much easier. Not only did Tom influence how I sold insurance, he also befriended me and met with me at different Round Table meetings to give me advice and encouragement. Tom has always been a leader in the industry and a hero to me.

Another friend I met through the Round Table was Hank McCamish who, in 1973, became its president. His system of being organized was of great help to me in devising my own methods. Hank came to Oregon at my request and spoke to our Annual Sales Congress. Then we had a great weekend in the mountains with our families skiing, having fun, and sharing ideas.

There were so many more learning experience for me at the MDRT meetings that I still consider those meetings, the ideas I gained, and the friends I made, to be the most significant, overall influence, in my entire career.

Not only did fellow members have their impact on me, but also did the leaders from other fields who were guest speakers at the meetings—people like Dr. Maxwell Maltz, the author of *Psychocybernetics,* and Bruce Jenner,

Olympic gold medalist.

Except for the Million Dollar Round Table, I would never have had the opportunity to keep on learning from the leaders.

Reflections

*A*s I look back over the years at the significant influence the Million Dollar Round Table and it members have had on me, I feel compelled to make one more attempt at encouraging you to partake of the significant benefits that await you.

The very least that will happen is that you will expand your horizons. And I guarantee that you will *always* get an idea at the annual meeting that will repay your expenditure of time and money

But more importantly, you will find your self being introduced to role models who will influence you to become the best you can become.

So let me give you one more O'Hearn truth:

To qualify for, and become a member of, and attend the annual meeting of the Million Dollar Round Table is one of the most important investments in your future that you can ever make.

Always seek more knowledge. It is the fountain of happiness.

"Before you score,
You must first have a goal."

Greek Proverb

CHAPTER 15

Giving Back

To make sure that I gave, as well as received, I tried to be of help to other agents. Three particular examples stand out in my memory.

The first example concerned a young friend of mine, from another company, who lived in Eugene, about 45 miles south of Albany. He had lots of talent but his work records indicated that he would have to make a substantial increase in effort if he was to be successful.

I decided that the first thing he needed to do was to prove to himself that he could accomplish everything that was necessary to get him to where he wanted to be. And, I wanted to prove to him that he could substantially increase his income and change his life if he would do just what I asked of him—for only three days each week. To prove this to him I made him promise to do whatever I said for the following three days.

First I told him that he was to set aside from five to

seven p.m. for each of the next three days to make phone calls to prospects. Then I told him that every time he dialed a prospect, and reached him, that he was to mark down eight dollars beside the name. That dollar amount, I told him, was how much money it was worth to him to just pick up the phone, dial it, and talk to a prospect. Next, he was to keep dialing the phone until he secured at least four appointments—keeping in mind that no matter how many times he had to dial, each time he reached the prospect, it was worth eight dollars—an amount that my own calls had been worth a few years before.

The idea that it might be worth that much money to just dial the phone really motivated him and, in the spirit of the game, he agreed to an all-out effort for the next three days. Here are the actual results of his effort.

Day	#Dialed	#Contacted	#Appointments
Tuesday	13	10	4
Wednesday	15	15	5
Thursday	15	12	4
Total:	43	37	13

At eight dollars per contact, he had earned $296 in our little game, and we both were confident that in thirteen appointments he would earn at least that much in commissions.

So my friend had proved to himself that he could do what it took if he was willing to discipline himself to make the calls. I would like to be able to say that he went on to great heights in the insurance business, but it was not to be so. For whatever reason, and I would guess it was the lack of a big enough dream, he went out of the business and on to something else before long. Without dreams this could be a tough business.

The second example concerned Bob Steinberg, a young agent for Western Life. I think the story is best told in Bob's own words:

"In 1967, when I was 26, I placed several cases in the same month and qualified for Western Life's Agent of the Month in the category of paid lives. As a result, I was awarded a trip to the home office in St. Paul, Minnesota, along with Bill O'Hearn, who had qualified as Agent of the Month in another category.

"One evening during that trip, while Bill and I were waiting for Bob Gallivan to join us for dinner, Bill asked me how I was doing during my first full year in the life insurance business. I replied that I thought I was doing quite well inasmuch as it looked like I would sell about $700,000 of volume by year end. I'm sure it was evident to Bill that the projected volume, along with qualifying for Agent of the Month, had me feeling pretty cocky about myself.

"Bill's response surprised me. He expressed that anything short of my qualifying for the Million Dollar Round Table during 1968 would be below my capabilities. I patiently explained to Bill that I was doing everything I knew how to produce as much as I was, and that, frankly, I didn't believe him. I couldn't even imagine increasing my production to MDRT level.

"Bill then asked me about my sales activity in terms of number of weekly interviews, sales, and average size case. After giving him these figures, he told me that if I followed his instructions, he would

guarantee my qualifying for the MDRT the following year.

"After doing some quick calculations on a cocktail napkin, Bill's simple instructions were to, 'Increase the number of weekly closing interviews from five to seven.' This seemed so simple that it was unbelievable. Nevertheless, I somehow worked up enough courage to commit to Bill that I would do this. I figured that if I did what he said and failed, it would be his fault, not mine.

"Upon returning to Portland, I began gearing up mentally for my new level of activity. Bill and I had agreed that I would keep a weekly scorecard, recording the number of calls, interviews, sales and the amount of volume and premium. At the conclusion of each week, I mailed the card to Bill in Albany, and he would periodically meet with me or write me a letter with words of advice, praise, or sometimes a reprimand.

"In addition to the scorecard, I also (at Bill's request) kept a notebook-sized piece of cardboard on which I drew squares. Each square represented one week. If at the end of a week I had achieved the seven closing interviews, I awarded myself a gold star on the appropriate square. If I failed to achieve that goal, I reluctantly pasted a red star on the square. The objective soon became to accumulate as many consecutive gold stars as possible, and keep to an absolute minimum the number of red stars. Although this may sound childish, it did serve as a motivator to me as I knew Bill would want to see the board whenever we got together.

"The end result was that I produced $1,017,000

and qualified for the 1968 Million Dollar Round Table.

"In retrospect, I learned several lessons from this experience. First of all, success is a relative term and has a wide range of definitions among individuals. How I viewed success that night in St. Paul, and how Bill measured success, were different. His vision for me was bigger than my vision for me. Secondly, higher levels of performance are achieved only after setting a goal, believing in the attainment of that goal, and committing oneself to its accomplishment. Thirdly, the goal must be reduced to small segments which can be frequently measured along the way. Finally, it is certainly helpful to have a mentor or support person who believes in you and takes a strong, sincere interest in your success. Bill O'Hearn was such a person. He contributed significantly to my success."

Bob Steinberg went on to have a tremendous career in not only the life insurance business, but also in the property and casualty insurance business. In 1985, Bob and his partner, Ron Packouz, sold their very profitable P&C business and today Bob is senior vice-president and chief administrative officer for the prestigious firm of Sedgwick James of Oregon.

I believe that one of the reasons for Bob's success during the period we worked together is reflected in a quote by Thomas Monson I read some twenty years later.

"When we deal in generalities, we shall never succeed. When we deal in specifics, we shall rarely have a failure.

*When performance is measured, performance
improves. When performance is measured and
reported, the rate of improvement accelerates."*

The third example happened earlier in my career
and involved one of my best friends, Bob Sederstrom. Bob
is gone now, but we were as close as two people could be.
He had come into the insurance business, at my urging, a
few years after I did and, because of our great friendship, I
made every effort to help him on his road to success. I
taught Bob what I had learned about the telephone
approach and the use of Al Granum's programming
system, but I didn't have to teach him how to work hard.
He *always* worked harder than I did. He was a navigator in
the Air Force during World War II and had graduated in
mathematics from the University of Oregon (I graduated in
history). So maybe it was not surprising that he had a more
business-like attitude about selling than I did. Not that he
wasn't enthusiastic. He was. He was just more—serious.

In 1961, Bob's fifth year in the business, I offered
to monitor his work effort. He was to keep exactly the
same kind of records as I kept, send me a monthly report
(he lived in Salem), and I would see how I could help him
to be more effective.

These were Bob's results in 1961:

Total Hours	2046
Field	1250
Office	715
Study	81
Calls	1721
Closing Interviews	257
Sales	60

It was obvious from my perspective that Bob sure didn't need to work any harder. But he could improve his ratio of interviews to calls, and sales to interviews. I also wanted him to change the kind of prospects he called on. He was a businessman and he should be calling on more businesses.

I also wanted him to grasp an O'Hearn "truth":

There is no virtue in hard work for the sake of working hard. There is virtue in hard work for the sake of effective results.

To bring this point home to him we examined my records for the year:

They looked like this:

Total Hours	1508
Field	533
Office	888
Study	87
Calls	878
Closing Interviews	174
Sales	77

Now if you were to put the calculator to the figures you would see that my ratio of calls to interviews was just a bit better than his, but that my closing ratio was about double. I believe that part of the reason was because I had developed a different philosophy—a different approach to the client. I thought in terms of a friend talking to a friend, and I think Bob, in these early years, kept the level of conversation more business-like. His way was no more wrong than mine was right. They were just different. But my closing ratio was better!

Two other things that were different between Bob and me in 1961—the dreams we held, and the size of our commission checks. You see I had a dream, a vision, of what I wanted to accomplish. Bob, at this early stage, just wanted to do a bit better each year.

I believe the difference between an exciting, energizing goal, and a desire to just get better each year was the difference between our earnings for the year. In today's dollars—$32,000.

So as you come up to your next goal setting session, how about getting a little less serious? How about taking the lid off your thinking.

How about imagining what you might dream if you knew you couldn't fail. And, how about remembering:

Whatever you believe is possible—is possible!!!

"The highest reward for man's toil
Is not what he gets for it,
But what he becomes by it."

John Ruskin

CHAPTER 16

Being Helped And Helping

From 1957 on, I needed help in reaching my objectives. For five of these years Gloria was my secretary. I'm not sure what kind of boss I was. I was probably more impatient with her than I would have been with someone else. Classic husband type.

But she was invaluable to me and helped make the insurance practice grow. My greatest strength was in calling on prospects and clients, and I disliked the details and paperwork that kept me from that. So I was always willing to give my wife, and other assistants later, as much responsibility as they were willing to accept, and I kept encouraging them to take on even more. By taking care of the details, they gave me time to do what I did best—sell.

Too often men and women in sales stymie their great talent by doing their own detail work. My advice to anyone who wants to advance his or her career in selling would be:

*The wisest and most profitable decision you can
make is to get great administrative help as soon as
possible.*

Having a good administrative staff also gave me the
time to become more involved in professional and
community groups. After serving as secretary of our local
life insurance association for two years, I went on to
become president. And I enjoyed being a member of
Kiwanis and helping with various fund raising projects.

The extra time generated also made it possible for
me to go skiing, golfing, hunting and to enjoy playing
more tennis and handball than I ever could have otherwise.
Top notch help led me to the discovery of another truth:

*Two people committed to working toward an
important goal are much more effective at reaching
that goal than one person alone.*

I didn't realize it at the time, but this truth was
going to become particularly important to me as I began to
gradually change the type of prospects I dealt with.

Another ally was the telephone. Using the phone
had always been an important part of my work effort, but
in the early years I had to struggle to make myself pick it
up. The effort it took just to take it off the cradle was
sometimes too much for me. I know now that my reluctant
attitude was transferred to the prospect at the other end of
the line. I *knew* he didn't want to talk to me, and he must
have sensed I wasn't happy about having to call him.

But when I finally developed a meaningful goal,
the telephone became a vital asset. When I made calls

because I *knew* I could help the prospect, I had a purpose bigger than my reluctance and my voice reflected my enthusiasm.

Even then, though, I had to teach myself to raise the level of enthusiasm for meeting the prospect. To do this, I used a simple technique. I placed a small mirror upright on my desk and as I started dialing the phone I practiced smiling into the mirror. Then when the prospect answered, I gave him the best smile I owned.

Now you are going to think I'm a little wacky, but I believe now that I was actually sending some form of electrical wave to the prospect. In some kind of subliminal sense, I was conveying that I was a warm, friendly, interesting guy to meet.

I'll never forget the meeting I had with a new prospect and his wife. He looked at me and said with a smile, "Do you want to know why I let you come talk to us tonight?"

Of course I did.

"I just wanted to see what someone looked like who talked to me on the phone like he had known me for 20 years."

I had to smile as I realized he was right. My attitude had penetrated the telephone.

I wasn't to understand until almost fifteen years later that I was applying a principle of success that has a psychological basis: "Act as if and it will be." The "As If" principle became part of my life, and is still an important part of my belief system today. I believe it was Dr. Norman Vincent Peale who said, "Act enthusiastic and you will become enthusiastic." I merely took that concept to my telephone approach and enjoyed the results.

I would urge you to consider something as simple as putting a mirror on your desk. You might find that you enjoy smiling to yourself. And I guarantee your prospect will enjoy receiving those warm, caring, sincere vibrations.

Eventually, I rarely made a cold call. Telephoning referred leads was much more powerful. It was also easier to pick up the phone, and prospects were more responsive to my approach when we had a common friend.

Bob Gallivan, author of, *How I Made $50,000 a Year Starting at Age 25,* was a master at obtaining referred leads—and developing long-term relationships. At his first meeting with a husband and wife, Bob got them to promise him two things. First, if they became clients of his that they would allow him to come back every year to review their program. Second, they would direct him to other friends whom he could help.

I was awed by the second part of this process. After his prospects had purchased insurance from him, Bob asked them to call their friends to make appointments for him—*while he waited.* Amazing! What was even more amazing was that they would do this for him. It's obvious why Bob went on to become one of the leading producers in the industry. I never had enough nerve to try his method. Asking for a referred lead that I would call on later was enough of a challenge for me. I needed a bigger dream if I were to duplicate Bob's system.

My telephone approach to a referred lead had stayed basically the same the previous few years. I would call the prospect and after mentioning our mutual friend's name, I would ask permission to visit in person for just a few minutes to show him what kind of insurance planning I did. I said that if I could help him, fine, and if I couldn't, that was fine too, but that at least we would become acquainted and I might be able to help him in the future.

In the initial interview, since I was mainly working in the family market, I always made it a point to talk to both the husband and the wife. The only items I took to that first meeting were a copy of a sample program in a nice binder and a yellow pad for notes.

I explained that I wanted to help them determine if their current insurance program was doing what they wanted and, more importantly, if they were paying the right amount for it. This point was my attention getter. I wanted them to think about how much money their insurance *should* be costing them. I found that most people wanted to verify that they were not paying too much for their current coverage. It was not a ploy on my part to determine if their present insurance was as good as mine. That was never a question since replacing a policy which had been sold by another agent was, during this era, unethical.

If my prospects decided they would like to see a program designed just for them, I guided them through the process of determining what they really wanted by following a format that would answer the questions in Al Granum's plan.

I put the figures I gathered from this conversation on a yellow pad in an order that my secretary understood. (She would later take the numbers and type the proposal after showing the rough copy to me to see if there were needed revisions). Before leaving the prospect, I would set up the next appointment when I would bring back their personalized program showing exactly how much insurance they should have based upon their stated objectives and exactly how much they should be paying for it.

I had known from 1957 on that if I were to advise other people on what was best for them, that I had to carry the ideal insurance program myself. I knew the kind of program I wanted if I died prematurely, or lived to the retirement years. It would be a program I would be proud to show a client, and even prouder to show my family. I decided to allocate 10 percent of my income to accomplish this. At one time (in today's dollars), my commissions were averaging $2,100 a month and my life insurance premium was $258 a month. My rule of thumb was: "If a prospect, or client, is paying more than I am, percentage-wise, they are paying too much." I never ran into anyone who was.

I developed my own guidelines for potential clients depending on their current salary or income. For average income families, my goal was to eventually get them to a minimum premium of six percent of gross salary. The percentage for those with higher incomes was eight to nine percent.

Many, if not most, of my prospects were not in a position to implement the ideal program immediately. My goal was to establish their objectives and then help them work towards reaching them. Because I was looking at the long term, my proposal, at the closing interview, always contained an illustration showing where I would like to see their program in five years. And, it gave us a good reason to get together for an update every year.

Selling in the personal market was very comfortable for me, however, it was important to my career growth that I call on more businesses and people with higher incomes. Receiving the title of Chartered Life Underwriter in 1963 had given me the self-esteem and credibility I thought I needed to make this move—a move that would take me from enthusiastic simplicity to complicated sophistication. From child to teenager. You know, when you think you know it all, and you try to make sure everyone else knows you know it all too.

Reflections

*H*ave you ever experienced a moment's hesitation when somebody asked you what you do for a living? Have you ever wished you could say something besides, "I sell life insurance?" In my early years I did. My image of what people thought of insurance agents was not exactly positive. And I ran into enough situations to keep reinforcing my belief.

What took me a long time to realize was that the people who held a low opinion of insurance agents, were not good prospects anyway. One of the great freedoms of the selling profession is that you have the right to choose the prospect with whom you'd like to deal. Yet, I was slow to learn how important we are to those who need us.

Over the years I had tried different titles on my letterhead and business cards to reinforce this need for approval: Estate Planner, Business Consultant, Estate Coordinator.

I finally came to realize that I sold life insurance to solve problems that could not be solved in any other way. And, I did it really well. All the fancy titles were just a smoke screen to make it easier to get in front of a prospect—and to make me feel more knowledgeable. And you know what? It didn't make it any easier—and I was already knowledgeable enough.

So accept who you are and what you do. Be proud. You don't need any cover-up to get an interview, or to put salve on your ego. You are enough just like you are. You have talent. You have a product. And there are people out there who need both your talent and your product.

It's okay to just tell it like it is!

It's commitment to excellence, not titles, that make you a success.

"The quality of a person's life is in direct
Proportion to his commitment to excellence.
Excellence can be obtained if you:
  Care more than others think is wise.
  Risk more than others think is safe.
  Dream more than others think is practical.
  Expect more than others think is possible."

                              Anonymous

CHAPTER 17

Riding The Crest

In 1964, I took a significant step toward working in the business and professional market: I opened an office in downtown Albany. Although I had a very nice office in a room over our garage at home, I figured a downtown location would be a more convenient and attractive place to meet current and prospective clients.

There were some beautiful old buildings right in the middle of our small town's business district. It was on the second floor of one of these that I decided to set up my office.

When I first looked at the office space it was a disaster area. It hadn't been occupied since World War II and it looked like it had been a casualty of that conflict. However, a well-known, creative interior designer assured me the location had great possibilities and that a renovation of the three rooms would not cost too much.

We decided that antiques, red carpet and flocked wallpaper of the "Old San Francisco" style would be in keeping with the building and would give me a first class office. The designer assured me he could pick up antiques at wholesale prices, and felt sure that the total costs would stay within the budget.

A realtor friend of mine, Rod Tripp, who owned the building made me a deal in which he would pay for the remodeling and then would charge me a base rent plus two and a half percent of the costs. If the costs stayed within the designer's estimate, that would work out to be $275 a month.

That much money would make a big dent in my monthly cash flow, but I was sure a prestigious office would bring in enough extra business to justify the expenditure. I forgot for the moment that increased sales were more a function of attitudes rather than appearances.

My designer would show me samples of carpet and wallpaper and ask me what I liked and I would always point out what appealed to me—assuming he was watching costs. How naive can a person be? In the end, the wallpaper alone cost as much as the original estimate for the entire decorating job, exclusive of antiques. By the time we finished, the added costs boosted my monthly rent from the anticipated $275 a month to $654 a month, which shook me up a bit then, and in 1993 dollars, $2,870 would still shake me up. Plus—I owed the bank for the antiques we had purchased. All that, and a five year lease.

A couple of years earlier I had predicted I could retire once my renewals reached $600 a month. So much for that plan. Some of my competitors wondered how I could be so ostentatious. I could have told them it was easy—just don't pay attention to details.

Perhaps it was a blessing in disguise because now I had no choice—I had to upgrade my prospecting. I could never pay for the office using my old methods. I must have been working towards what has become another O'Hearn truth:

Risk is absolutely necessary if you are to grow towards your potential.

About the time I moved into my new office, I opened what was, to me, a gigantic case. Perhaps it was coincidence. Perhaps panic over the rent pushed me into looking at *everyone* as a prospect although I thought I had been doing that. Whatever it was, I contacted an older businessman whom I had met at various social and civic functions. He was a stockholder in a successful business in Salem. The firm had built up a great following of customers over the years, their reputation was impeccable, and business was good.

In our initial meetings it became clear that the owners had done almost no insurance planning. I was to find that their situation was not unique in the business world.

After several meetings the problem was narrowed down to the one that would cause the most significant impact in case of death of any one of the three partners (I am using the word partner interchangeably, although it was a corporation and they were stockholders, not partners): There was no buy-sell arrangement. This meant that in the case of the death of a stockholder, his share would pass directly to his heirs via his will. I asked if this result would cause a problem and everyone agreed it would. It would, in their eyes, not be favorable to end up in business with heirs who knew nothing about the inner workings of the business.

The solution of course was to have their attorney draft an agreement by which the surviving stockholders, or the corporation, could purchase the stock. That left only one other potential problem. Where would the money come from to purchase the stock? Would that be a problem? They agreed it would.

My solution, naturally, was to have the corporation secure enough insurance on each stockholder to provide the necessary money in the event of the death of any one of them. The trouble with my solution was that it would create havoc with their cash flow. In other words, they couldn't afford the solution. It was a "damned if they did and damned if they didn't" situation.

They finally resolved that they would take it one step at a time and insure the oldest partner first, figuring that he was probably their most imminent risk.

The senior partner took the required physical and I submitted an application to Western Life for $200,000— the amount the surviving partners would need to buy out the oldest partner's share in the event of his death. Despite the man's age and the potential for insurability problems— which could have resulted in an even higher premium and more selling on my part—the company underwriters issued the policy at a standard rate.

I was on Cloud Nine. Up to this point, I had not spent any time thinking about my potential commission. I rarely did. Thinking about how much I would earn on a case, I had discovered, interfered with my ability to be objective about my client's problems. But now that I was about to complete this case, I allowed myself to think, "Wow!" Never before had I been in a situation where I could earn a commission of almost $10,000.

Nice dream while it lasted. The partners got cold feet, and the amount of the premium loomed larger than the threat of a payoff in case of death. They knew they had a problem, and that insurance was the answer, but they could not bring themselves to accept the cost of insuring the entire amount. So, in spite of my best arguments to the contrary, the partners elected to insure the senior partner for just a fraction of the problem. They decided to take only $44,000 of the $200,000, and accept having to face the consequences.

To say I was upset would be an understatement. But it was not about the loss of potential commission. I had really become involved in this case, and I just could not see that partial coverage was going to be any kind of a solution. I felt as if I had not really done my job.

But I had learned these very important lessons that were to stand me in good stead over the coming years:

1. No matter how great I perceived the client's problem to be, he is not going to solve it unless the fear of loss is greater that the fear of the cost.

2. What I would do, and what the client would do are very possibly two different things.

3. No matter how big the case, it isn't done until it's done, and I better not count my chickens (commissions) before they are hatched (received).

Two interesting sidelights to the above case occurred after it was finally completed. One happened immediately afterwards and took me by surprise. For reasons that are beyond me, the potential commission that I had almost made was immediately forgotten. I did not have one minute of regret for what might have been. This attitude, wherever it came from, was to serve me well in the years to come.

The second sidelight occurred three years later when the senior partner died having suffered multiple illnesses. I delivered the check for $44,000, and it was appreciated, but it was a drop in the bucket compared to the problems the remaining partners were facing. Since the stockholders were now concerned with finding cash to buy out the estate, and not concerned with the need for insurance, I was not brought into their planning. And I really don't know what happened except that it was only a few years before the company was no longer in business. Would the entire $200,000 have made a difference in the long run? I don't know. It might have—but it was too late to cry—the milk had already been spilled.

However, this experience did lend power to my closing skills. In the future, I did everything I could to convince a client not to settle for partial solutions.

Through this case and several others I learned another truth:

There is no need for me to ever be concerned about how much money I would make on a particular case.

If I did a good job, the commissions would come, if not from this case then from the next.

The law of averages will always work out!

Reflections

*W*hile the 1960s were wonderful years, I realize now that I spent a great deal of it resting on my laurels. I was meeting my goals but I was coasting, albeit at a very nice level.

I did have one short burst of intense energy when I set a goal to sell $1,000,000 of insurance in 90 days. I made my goal, but what stands out most in my mind about that time was the ice cold shower I took each morning after my regular shower. I figured that if I could start out each morning doing something I absolutely did not want to do, that the rest of the day would be a piece of cake. This proved to be true. But I never made another Spartan commitment like that again.

But, I was beginning to forget Grant Taggart's lesson. I seemed to be running faster and faster. I had turned up the power on the treadmill with no clear idea why. I was now just a businessman doing more business.

There were no quantum leaps in my life, and consequently no quantum results. I was just slugging it out. Well—I've got to admit—I was having a little fun.

I remember meeting in my beautiful San Francisco look-alike office with Bill and Irene Coburn, who were close friends, as well as good clients. Bill and Irene had brought their CPA along to listen to my ideas about their need for business life insurance. As we neared the end of my presentation, I still hadn't recognized any good buying signs from anyone. Bill and Irene kept looking at their CPA, and he kept being very noncommittal.

So, I decided to have some fun.

The round conference table we were seated at had a spring-loaded adjustable height feature. By moving a lever, which was situated underneath, the top of the table would rise to a higher position.

So I said to Bill and Irene, and the stubborn CPA, "Let's try something. Let's all put our hands on top of the table, and see if we can get some kind of sign that you should go ahead with my ideas." They looked at me as if I were a little crazy, but I persisted so they reluctantly put their hands, palms down, on the table. Then I said, "Now let's just concentrate for a minute and see if we can discover any sign." I didn't have enough nerve to ask them to close their eyes.

At this point, unobtrusively, I pushed my knee against the lever.

I cannot describe the look of shock and disbelief that came across those three faces as the top of table began to rise. I could only look serious for a few moments as I asked if they were now convinced they should buy—and then I almost fell out of my chair laughing.

Needless to say, the mood got lighter, the CPA even laughed, and I got the sale. Can't say I ever used that close again, but it was sure fun that time.

So, once in awhile, let the leprechaun in you come out. It's good for a laugh—and maybe a sale.

Have some fun every single day of your life.

"This vision that you glorify in your mind,
This ideal that you enthrone in your heart—
This you will build your life by,
This you will become."

James Allen

CHAPTER 18

Complicated Sophistication Versus Mature Simplicity

After experiencing a taste of insurance planning in the business world, I wanted to keep calling on high income prospects. However, we didn't have a lot of those kind of businesses in our small town, and even though I had closed one big case I still had no clear idea of how to approach Mr. Big. Nor did I know what I would say if I were successful in securing the appointment. I found this concern to be a great ally to call reluctance. My rationale was that: "Maybe I should spend more time getting smarter before I make a call."

It would take me a while to realize that prospects with money are not much different than prospects without money. They just have bigger problems to solve—and that a nice side benefit of solving bigger problems was a better payoff for my efforts.

To give you an idea of how much better, the

following is a comparison of the results of 1958 and 1966:

Effort	1958	1966
Calls per week	32	20
Closing interviews/wk	6	5
Hours per week	42	?

Results		
Sales per month	10	12
Volume per month	$175,950	$350,000
Closing ratio	1 to 2.6	1 to 1.7

Value of each call	$8.15	$38.25
Value of each interview	$43.63	$153

There is a lesson or two here. One is that working in a higher income market has significant benefits. The second is: Can you imagine what the results would have been if I had matched my 1958 work effort of calls? Resting on laurels can be expensive.

Once I became somewhat successful in approaching higher income prospects, using basically the same telephone approach I had always used, I discovered that if I would ask good questions during the initial interview, and let the prospect do most of the talking, the prospect himself would uncover the problem that needed my type of solution.

In the beginning I thought I could solve a business prospect's problems by showing him how smart I was. I would overwhelm him with a 15 to 20-page proposal in a fancy cover. However, the only person I was impressing was me. I was not impressing the prospect and I was definitely *not* impressing my secretary. Even though the majority of the verbiage was in fact boiler plate, every page had to be typed as an original copy. And instead of solving the prospect's problem, I found I was adding to it.

Eventually I learned that the more simply I could explain to myself what I was trying to accomplish, the more simply I could explain it to the prospect. In time this led to the development of my Five-Pager. It looked like this:

Page 1	Prospect's Name
Page 2	Your situation today
Page 3	What you said you want to accomplish
Page 4	The problem (the difference between Page 2 and Page 3)
Page 5	The solution

I reduced the information on each page to as few words as possible. I learned this kind of streamlining from Eli Morgan, one of the most innovative and creative insurance producers I have ever known.

I had been calling on a wealthy lumberman, and presenting various ideas without success, for about eight years. These ideas were never comprehensive. I was offering solutions without really understanding the problem. I finally asked him if I could bring Eli down to talk to him, explaining that Eli was an expert in helping people like him solve estate planning problems. He agreed to the meeting and what evolved over the next nine months was a series of complicated fact finding interviews with the prospect, his CPA, his attorney, Eli's CPA and attorney, Eli and me.

Basically the problem turned out to be one of

arranging the estate so that the prospect's wife and children would be well taken care of, the business assets would be properly liquidated, and sufficient cash would be available to pay estate taxes.

With all of us present at the closing interview, Eli was ready. Our proposal had been narrowed down to as few words as possible on only three pieces of paper. Eli had these three pages enlarged to 30" by 30" and mounted on cardboard which he presented on a stand-up easel. The pages were titled as follows:

Page 1   Here is where you are now
Page 2   Here is what you said you want to do
Page 3   Here is how you do it

It was beautiful in its simplicity and beautiful in its results. The client's estate was arranged exactly as he wanted it, Eli and I had a new client, and I had my first million dollar case. My share of the commission, over $10,000, amounted to more money than I had made in my first three years combined.

This case presented a critical juncture in my career. I could have said, "From now on I'm only working on the Biggies." But in looking back at the past nine months of effort on this case I realized that until the very last day when our prospect finally said "yes," he could have just as easily said "no." He could have gotten tired of the whole process, or gotten up on the wrong side of the bed one morning, and said, "Forget it." Several months of work would have gone down the drain with no income to show for it.

So I made a wiser decision. I decided, that in the future, I would always do just what I had done while this case was in progress. During the nine months on this case I had continued my current work pattern and did everything just as if there was no big case involved. Consequently, my income without the big case was at the level it needed to be. The fact that the bonus came through was great, but had it not I still would have had a great year and it would have been business as usual. I decided that was the way I would work in the future—business as usual, and let the bonus cases fall where they may.

I was lucky. Some salespeople get hooked on the dream of a big commission and drop their daily commitment to produce. That is a great way to go broke. Eli, however, was one of a kind. He focused only on the big cases, the kind my friend Dave Tangvald said you could run out of by noon in Portland, Oregon. Eli's rare combination of talent and drive eventually made him one of the biggest producers in the country. Eli's way was right for him. My way worked out great for me.

Reflections

Several years ago I invited Tom Wolff to come to talk to the Portland Life Underwriters. His career was a model for everyone and his Capital Needs Analysis program was being used by thousands of insurance sales people.

I especially remember one principle he talked about. It was the KISS principle, which had been interpreted to mean: "Keep it simple stupid." Tom's version of KISS meant "Keep it simple—and sincere." I liked that.

The concept of keeping it simple was never more pronounced than in the questions and statements the great Ben Feldman came up with. There was genius in his method. If I recall correctly he used to paste a $1,000 bill over the top of several $20, $50, and $100 bills, on the opening page of his presentation kit. On top of the $1,000 bill he pasted three pennies. While visiting with a prospect Ben would intrigue him with a statement like, "This is what I sell—these kind of dollars for pennies apiece." I can't speak for the prospect, but I'll tell you, it impressed me. I'd never even seen a $1,000 bill!

Have you looked lately at what kind of questions you are asking prospects? And what kind of statements you are making? Have you stepped back and looked at what you are saying through the eyes of the prospect? Is there something you are doing or saying that could be made simpler? It has been my experience that even the wealthy prospects know far less than we sometimes assume.

Many years ago I was calling on the executive vice-president of one of our biggest companies in Oregon. He was a nice man and very astute. I was explaining an idea to him that made perfect sense to me when he stopped me and said, "Bill, would you please explain term insurance to me?" I couldn't believe my ears. I thought everyone knew what term insurance was. He didn't. He had never been given an explanation of term insurance, or whole life for that matter. From that day on I tried to quit making assumptions about what I thought my prospects knew and didn't know.

Are you selling from ledger statements? Do you believe this is the simplest way to explain your product? If so, maybe you should consider rethinking why a prospect buys. Ledger statements do not create excitement. They do not arouse feelings. Ledger statements appeal to logic. People buy from emotion. Ledger statements explain "How"—not "Why."

I urge you to review some of Ben Feldman's Million Dollar Round Table talks. Or read his book, *The Feldman Method*. Study the kind of questions he asks. Then ask yourself, "What can I do or say to make my approach, my presentation, and my close so simple that it has genius?" You'll be amazed at what you come up with.

Always have at least one big case in the hopper, but don't spend a second worrying about it.

"Our duty as human beings
Is to proceed as if limits
To our abilities do not exist."

Anonymous

CHAPTER 19

Some Forks In The Trail

By the mid-1960s the world was my oyster. I had a wonderful family, a good business and good friends. My family and I enjoyed plenty of recreation and time together, and I loved my work. I wouldn't have been in any other field. I was in the top two percent of insurance producers in the world and in the top three percent of income earners in the United States. I was living the American Dream. So how come I felt so unfulfilled?

I wasn't to discover for many years that the pursuit of *More-Bigger-Better* was not exactly what a full life was all about. So, in the meantime, I decided to do just the opposite of what might get whatever was nagging at me to go away. I would get bigger. I would work smarter and sell larger policies. That would be challenging and maybe I would feel better.

About this time, many insurance companies were

telling their agents that they (the agents) needed to expand their operation and become a one-stop-shop. They said we would have to get involved in property and casualty insurance, disability insurance, health insurance, and the securities business if we were to survive. Most of us were really happy just selling life insurance—but what did we know? I finally acquiesced, partially, and decided to get into the securities business. I was already a good insurance advisor and I could be a good financial advisor as well. It seemed like a logical way to help my clients and increase my income at the same time. It didn't occur to me that being involved in securities would take time away from selling insurance.

Even though I received my securities license, I didn't do anything with it for a while. But it did feel good to be able to say, "Yes, I am licensed to sell securities." It kind of made me feel more—professional? In retrospect, it was just an ego stroker.

Then mutual funds started to get really popular. A few of my peers around the country were doing quite well selling them in addition to insurance. Why not me? The way things were going in the economy, it looked like a *sure* way to make money. I discovered one particular fund that stood out. It was a phenomenal performer and had led the field during the past couple of years. It was a top recommendation by the experts. How could anyone miss with a deal like that?

Although I wasn't investing myself, I convinced my folks and one of my very best clients that this particular mutual fund was worth investing in. My enthusiasm convinced my folks to take $25,000 out of savings and my friend borrowed a substantial amount from his insurance program—something I wasn't comfortable with, but this was such a good deal...! I could just see them making a bunch of money. I would be a hero and my new additional career would be launched.

How come some people are blessed with great timing and others are not? The Gods of Fortune must have been frowning the day I decided to sell securities. This phenomenal mutual fund stopped performing almost the same day of the sale. In fact it dropped so low, there was no hope of doing anything but hanging on. It only took ten years for it to come back up to the price my folks and friend paid for it. From hero to goat in one fell swoop. My securities career ended the day it started. I thought of the whole experience as the, "Great Mutual Fund Fiasco."

Shortly after, another coincidence changed my life forever. I met Hal Nutt, a well known educator from Purdue University. Hal was a combination of great teacher and early day Zig Ziglar—southern accent and all.

Most of my insurance colleagues and I had attended his two and three day seminars on business insurance and estate planning, and all of us were inspired by his knowledge and enthusiasm. His Hellfire and Brimstone approach to a prospect translated into "I care about you and your problems, and I may be able to help, so let's sit down and talk, and let the results be what they will be."

Needless to say, I looked up to Hal and I was honored to be selected to be his host when he came to Portland to be the featured speaker at the annual Portland Sales Congress in 1969.

I picked Hal up at the airport the night before the meeting, took him to Portland's best hotel and made sure he was comfortable. We stayed up talking and late that evening, Hal Nutt, the teacher, the sage, the big name in the industry said to me, "How would you like to be president of an insurance company?"

I assumed he was joking with me, but I asked him to repeat his question anyway. He was dead serious. It was as if he had peeked into my secret list of dreams. For years I had fantasized about being president of a company.

Hal told me about a Canadian company which was successfully marketing an innovative insurance idea. Starting a similar company in Oregon using this idea would present a great opportunity for both Oregon policyholders and stockholders. He asked me to fly to Calgary at the expense of the Canadian company to see if I liked the idea and would consider being the spearhead for a similar company in Oregon.

Hal said he would be glad to serve on the board of directors of the Oregon company—as he did in Canada. I was faced with the possibility of making a dream come true. Talk about a pump up in ego. Would I let the company fly me back to see their operation? Would I ever!!!

And so began my journey into "The Great Detour."

*"Nurture your mind with great thoughts;
To believe in the heroic makes heroes."*

Benjamin Disraeli

CHAPTER 20

Which Direction?

Calgary, Alberta, sitting amongst the unbelievably beautiful Canadian Rockies. A place you dream about going to on vacation, and here I was, taking the biggest ego trip of my life with all expenses paid. However, the experience I was about to get involved in was not going to be a vacation, and in retrospect might possibly be compared to jumping out of an airplane and free falling for several thousand feet—tremendously exhilarating I would imagine, until you discovered you weren't wearing a parachute.

The insurance company I visited was just a few years old, but was running on a track of tremendous enthusiasm. The management had designed a unique life insurance product for people 35 years old, and younger, which was the best I had ever seen. It was a policy that started with a base of permanent insurance with excellent cash values and had a fixed premium of $360 a year regardless of the age of the insured. The policy had several options which young people could select as they reached certain stages in their lives. These options allowed for the permanent portion of the policy to decrease slightly while adding term insurance for additional protection. These options could be exercised in the event of marriage, the purchase of a home or birth of children. The most unique feature of the policy was that the cost never changed. It stayed at $360—*A dollar a day.* The dollar a day cost had a nice sound to it, and I could envision tremendous possibilities for an agency force of young people selling to young people, along with a great financial opportunity for potential stockholders.

The key question for me, however, was whether or not I was willing to give up what I was doing so successfully and start in a new direction. That was what this initial trip was all about, and what my hosts hoped to convince me to do.

The Canadian company's proposal was that they would provide detailed instructions for raising the initial capital, actuaries for getting the special policy approved in Oregon, and help in recruiting and training new agents. They had the system pretty well worked out, since it had not been too long since they had gone through the initial process with their company. In exchange for their guidance they would take a founder's stock position in the Oregon company, and have Hal Nutt and the president of the Canadian company serve on the board of directors.

It all sounded exciting, but I decided to go home and talk to a few people I knew to be solid businessmen before I made up my mind. Prior to leaving however, the president had me sit in on agent training sessions, talk to policyholders and stockholders, and take an in-depth look at everything the company was doing so I would be fully informed. They also had me spend a great deal of time studying the special policy and how the cash values and dividends worked to make it such an exciting product for those selling it and those buying it. I was impressed!

The next couple of months were hectic. Dozens of questions had to be answered. How would we start? Would it work? What was the investment possibility? Could we find enough new agents? Would Oregonians be interested in supporting a new company?

Not every one I talked to was positive. More than one friend questioned why I would want to give up such a successful life for what looked like such a big risk. The Chairman of the Board of Western Life, Bob Richardson, advised me against starting the company. He said I had no idea what I would be getting into and on a personal note said that, "Making Bill O'Hearn the president of a life insurance company would be like capturing a wild bird and making it live in a cage." But this admonition came from the same man who said I couldn't become successful in the insurance business and have time for golf. Bob was a sniper in World War II, and an actuary. I should have known he wouldn't miss twice in a row.

However, as I talked to more and more friends about the possibilities of this exciting opportunity, the majority became more and more enthusiastic. Yet something was holding me back. It wasn't the idea of hard work. I was used to that, although I suspected this challenge might be bigger than anything I had ever tackled. And I was absolutely convinced that my stock in the new company, for which I would have to borrow the money to buy, would be worth two or three million dollars in a few short years. So how come I was hesitating?

I still hadn't identified the source of the restlessness I had been feeling for the past few years, and I wasn't sure whether this new idea would decrease or increase this feeling. I did realize that my life style would have to change. My Thursdays off would go out the window. The freedom of skiing over fifty days a year would have to come to an end for a while along with the golf. Hopefully, I could still could find time to play tennis and handball.

Giving up my free time was certainly a drawback. Would becoming rich be worth it? I knew it probably would not. I had skied next to millionaires for years in Sun Valley and they weren't having any more fun than I was. So what good reason was there to take on this big adventure? The fact that it was adventurous was a plus. The excitement of doing something that was different but still in my field was tremendously appealing.

I finally decided that I would not take on this project unless I could find a better reason than the obvious ones. My decision had to have roots in something other than ego and money. But what?

Then it came to me that this opportunity might afford me the chance to have a positive effect on the lives of the agents we would recruit. To find young men and women not already in the insurance business, and teach them how to sell and become successful felt right to me. The idea that I might be a motivating force in their lives became the pivotal point for my decision to form the new life insurance company. Had I only known then what the future would hold.

My last effort at personally producing life insurance sales in 1969 came at the end of August. From

September on, my entire focus and energy were concentrated on the formation of the new company. Yet my insurance income for the year including renewals was $55,000, which translated into today's dollars is over $250,000. Things had been going pretty darned good!

I had become an expert at one thing, how to sell life insurance to solve business and estate problems. Now I was heading at a right angle to my talent—and my experience.

Remember the trap I mentioned in an earlier chapter about—if something is working, stop and start doing something else?

I was about to spring the trap.

"*You don't fail at anything.*
You produce results with everything.
It's what you do with those results
That determines the champions
Or the also-rans."

Anonymous

CHAPTER 21

The Great
Detour

If I had had the slightest clue as to the amount of combined effort so many great friends and associates would have to put forth to start an insurance company, I doubt I would ever have taken that first step.

But I did, and for the next nineteen months we put in a Herculean effort fulfilling the requirements of the Corporation Commissioner, the Insurance Commissioner, and raising the money for the stock—$1,500,000—in the midst of a major recession.

We finally hit our stock pledge goal when fifty prominent Albany businessmen, in a show of great support, put in $5,000 apiece to put us over the top—a fact that would come back to haunt me.

On April 3, 1971, Columbia Life Insurance Company became a reality. My feelings at that moment reflected one of the all time highs of my life. I was the president of a new and exciting life insurance company.

Now all we had to do was to prove to the world that our enthusiasm was well placed.

Over the next year and a half, excitement reigned supreme. We recruited eighty-five young men and women, trained them in solid sales techniques, had motivating sales rallies, and watched a tremendous esprit de corps develop between all involved. Unfortunately, our sales force created more enthusiasm than it did sales. They reminded me of me in the early days.

In retrospect I can see that we probably failed to make enough sales because, in complying with state requirements, the emphasis in our special policy had changed from the accumulation of cash to a more traditional needs basis policy. Even though our policy was special, it was definitely not as exciting as our Canadian counterpart's. And, as we consequently learned, turned out to be more difficult to sell.

In the meantime, our capital base was eroding and we began to realize that we weren't turning the corner fast enough. In order to make sure that we did not get into an impaired position, the board decided to seek a merger.

An agreement with a Utah life insurance company was eventually put together. Our stockholders received shares in the Utah company, which was worth only a fraction of the original price if sold immediately, but still appeared to be the best bet, for the long run, of anything we had looked at. There were lots of glowing promises made, especially as to my future, but once the merger was complete, the Utah company gave notice to our home office staff, released our entire agency force, and absorbed our remaining cash of $750,000. And, within three months, in spite of an *ironclad* employment agreement, I was out of a job.

And so the dream ended. And an expensive dream it was—financially and mentally. I had accepted a salary significantly below my cash flow requirements during the previous three and one half years, knowing that eventually I would gain it back. I had gambled in a high stakes game—and lost.

I was left with nothing but the equity in our home. But that was just a circumstance. Given time I could regain the dollars. What I did not have time to do was gain back the money for my children's college education. They were going to have to borrow and work their way to a degree—which all of them did.

My family had to pay a bigger price than I could have anticipated. My priorities had become confused, and my children, particularly my young son, Chip, had seen little of me during this time. I had forgotten what was important.

Reflections

Looking back from a perspective of twenty years later there are so many significant lessons I learned from the Columbia Life adventure. For one thing, after the experience of stockholder meetings, board meetings, rallies, and banquets, I had gained in ability to make a presentation to any size group. I felt confident in talking to anyone.

I also learned a great deal more about people. Some good, some not so good. And I learned a whole bunch about humility and fallibility.

But probably the biggest lesson I learned, and very likely the most expensive was this: It only takes a short while to fragment the work of years. When I changed my focus from helping my clients to trying to build a life insurance company I began to pay less attention to relationships that had taken years to build. I had turned some of my bigger clients over to other insurance men since these clients needs were sometimes more volatile, but even the smaller clients had needs that I wasn't getting to. In many cases, I was never able to regain our pre-Columbia Life rapport.

So my first plea to you is to never let anything distract you from what you do best—uncovering problems and offering solutions. Don't let perceived big gains or a big ego throw you off track.

A close friend of mine, a highly successful life insurance salesman, was riding along on a high crest when an opportunity to invest in a business he knew nothing about came to him. It appeared to have a significant chance for gain. Within two years the economy went soft, the $125,000 he had in his bank account soon disappeared, and he found himself holding the tab for a $500,000 note he had guaranteed.

By virtue of his great ability to sell, the liquidation of some hard earned assets, and his forcibly learned ability to go without, he was finally able to pay everything off. The debt went away in five years. The pain still remains..

So beware of *great opportunities*. Professionally, personally and financially it might prove too expensive.

"He who gains victory
Over all men is strong:
But he who gains a victory
Over himself is all powerful"

Lao-Tse

CHAPTER 22

Seeking A
New Direction

The loss of Columbia Life seemed so immense, I felt I had hit rock bottom. From insurance company president back to agent in one short fall. It seemed like a huge demotion. I realize now that my perspective was warped, but it was nevertheless real in my mind at the time. Also real in my mind was the concern: "How could I advise people about their financial situation when I had made such a mess of my own?"

The only thing I had done really right financially in all the previous years was to put 10 percent of my income into my insurance program. In my discouraged state I let my CPA convince me to surrender all my permanent policies because of the large loan against them—the cash values had been among the assets I had used to make up for the reduction in my income during Columbia Life. From his perspective it was sound advice, but I never should have listened. Somehow, I could have found a way to pay back the money. Never again could I get such favorable rates and such significant annual increases in cash value. The impact of that loss would not really hit home for a few years.

I gave up my downtown office and moved everything home. Gloria and I had managed to keep the bills pretty much up to date during the Columbia Life experience by liquidating assets, but now I was about one month's income away from panic.

I started making insurance calls—very reluctantly. Several of Columbia Life's stockholders were also my clients, but I felt that some would not be too eager to see me. That was probably more in my mind than theirs, but it did exert a major influence on whom I called. Talk about call reluctance.

I had lost my confidence, and I felt the need for moral support, so I decided to look for a general agent who would take me under his wing and coach me back to big production. I can't imagine now why I felt I needed this. I knew the path to success in the insurance business as well as anyone. Maybe I just needed someone to remind me.

Walt Kelly, one of the finest men I have ever known and general agent for Massachusetts Mutual, tried to help. He assigned me his right-hand man, George Evans, as an extra guide and even sent me to a week-long pension school to see if that was what I wanted to do. Good accountants make good pension administrators. I could have sold pensions, but I never could have serviced them. All Walt's efforts were to no avail. As my cousin is prone to say, "You can always tell an Irishman, but you can't tell him much." I had been my own boss for too long, and even though I thought I wanted help, I didn't want it bad enough to follow directions.

Then I joined forces with Dick Carney, a big hitter from a Salem, who had taken care of a couple of my larger clients during my time with Columbia Life. We planned to put together a *super agency* with two other good producers, Bob Carey and Bob Sederstrom. They finally went on without me. Everybody was in a producing mood but me.

There was no question about my staying in the insurance industry, but I couldn't seem to force myself to go back to doing the specific things that had made me successful. Especially my Friday-for-planning sessions. I was tired, and just thinking about the concentrated effort made me more so.

But work I did. I made no great effort but I did manage to pay the bills—barely.

About this time, I talked with a friend of mine, Frank O'Brien, a general agent for another large insurance company. He had been to a highly motivating seminar a few months before and he thought the experience would do me a world of good and give me back some positive perspective. He insisted I go and even paid for it and let me pay him back later.

The seminar, called Omega, was an intensive four day learning experience on how to take charge of your life. The seminar helped me realize that the direction of my future was up to me—that it was my responsibility to choose that direction and not sit around and let it happen. I came away from those four days with a renewed spirit, a new set of lifetime goals, and a determination to use my new-found knowledge to grow towards my potential.

I was tremendously excited about what Omega was teaching, but I also sensed that follow-up sessions would be extremely important. So I wrote them and offered to help organize graduates into ongoing support groups. They didn't seem interested so in my ongoing quest for personal growth I asked Dr. Ed Timmons, a well known psychologist, from Louisiana State University, whom I had heard talk at a MDRT meeting, to come to Oregon and put on his human development seminar for a group of Oregon's leading life insurance producers. He agreed and, a few months later, twenty-four of us gathered for an intense three and one-half days of learning.

Many good things came from that seminar, including a special camaraderie among the participants. The greatest gift for me, however, was seven words that changed my life. I'd like to share those words with you:

Then is Then
and
Now is Now

This uncomplicated advice allowed me to finally put things in perspective and to let go of the past. Thank you, Ed Timmons, you made a difference in my life.

I also learned that continued personal growth would be a necessary, and important part of my life forever. Remember the saying, "He teaches that which he most needs to learn?" Four years later I formed the Alpha Learning Institute. Alpha seemed an appropriate name since it symbolizes the beginning, and that's what I wanted to offer to people. I wanted to help others advance on their journey by teaching them how to let go of the limiting experiences of their past, and to live for the now by developing winning attitudes and setting exciting goals for the future.

The Alpha seminars were an avocation. Life

insurance was my vocation. I held the seminars on weekends at various resorts in Oregon, and concentrated on the insurance business during the week.

Alpha was fulfilling for me, but I was still seeking a track to run on in my profession. But as another saying goes, "When the student is ready, the teacher will appear."

About this time I met Bob Daniel, who had developed a sophisticated method for people to maximize their existing life insurance coverage by leveraging cash values in their current policies to create more death benefit, and eventually significantly more cash values—without additional premiums. The plan was designed so that the prospective client would borrow on his present cash value and put part of that value into annuities and part into premium for additional insurance. The key to the whole program was the ability of annuities to pay more interest than the cash value in the policy, and the deductibility, under the law, of interest paid on policy loans.

Cash values in insurance policies had always been a sacred cow. It was an unwritten rule that you just didn't touch them. I had been in business 27 years and had never replaced a policy that I or any one else had sold—and I wasn't about to start now. When Bob showed me how current policies would stay in force, yet be the means by which clients could add more insurance and build bigger cash values, I was interested.

I looked at the idea from every angle. It could help my clients, present and future. There was a small drawback. The system required a $60,000 investment on my part for computer, software and supplies. I didn't have any money, but I did have equity in my home that I could borrow against. A wise financial advisor would have probably told me not to do that—not because the program wasn't valid, but because I was gambling a good portion of the last resource I had available.

My CLU peers were not impressed with my idea. They saw it as "raiding" cash values. I viewed it differently and felt I was following the CLU Professional Pledge, which said "—I shall, in the light of all conditions surrounding those I serve, which I shall make every conscientious effort to ascertain and understand, render that service which, in the same circumstances, I would apply to myself."

I was making suggestions to people about how to use their cash values better, something I really believed was best for the them, and although I never replaced a single policy, the idea rubbed many agents the wrong way. I can understand how they felt. Had it been their idea instead of mine, I might not have thought it was so great either.

As it turned out, Bob Daniel's program was the forerunner of Universal Life which appeared on the insurance scene a short time later. Possibly because it was the insurance industry itself which introduced Universal Life, it was embraced by most insurance people as the greatest thing since sliced bread.

In the meantime, I liked Bob's idea so well I decided to take the next step in my career. I became a general agent—and went another sixty thousand dollars in debt. No one has ever accused me of being conservative.

"I know God will not give me
Anything I can't handle.
I just wish He didn't trust me
So much."

Mother Teresa

CHAPTER 23

Another Path

In the process of getting prepared to bring other agents into my agency, I began to test market the new plan myself to see the reaction of prospects. Fortunately for me, my oldest daughter, Molly, was working with me and she took on the job of becoming computer literate with Bob Daniel's system. Without her I couldn't have operated. Computers, I thought at the time, took a different talent than I owned, and I had absolutely no desire to make the effort it would require to become proficient.

So, thanks to Molly, I began to open cases, gather the necessary information from the prospect and then turn over all the work to her. This task involved contacting companies in which the prospect owned policies and obtaining the information needed for the system. It was time consuming, but Molly was great at details and in no time I was ready to make actual presentations.

The reaction of the people I talked to was exciting.

The idea of obtaining more life insurance, and significantly more cash value at retirement without an increase in current outlay really got their attention. The education process of exactly how it worked was more detailed than in a conventional insurance sale, but once the prospect understood, the sale followed almost automatically.

I became so enthusiastic about what I was doing that two of my friends, Gary Bold, a pharmacist, and Doug Carl, a CPA, decided they would like to join me in what appeared to be an excellent opportunity to create significant insurance sales by selling individually and helping to build the general agency. Even though they knew nothing about selling life insurance, they understood this new idea and felt they could convince people they knew to increase their insurance program without increasing their cost.

We set up an office in the finished basement of my home and began to make calls. It was working and we were charged. I started calling on agents whom I knew around the state and soon we had a few more enthusiastic people. It wasn't long before we decided that we needed a downtown office and that Gary and Doug should be partners in the general agency. The three of us went to the bank and told my banker what we had in mind and he agreed to lend us $75,000 based upon our current sales results.

It wasn't too long before we had ten agents in our agency and an overhead of $18,000 a month. If each agent merely made a living with the idea we were in great shape.

Have you ever wondered if sometimes your timing is just not right? Our whole concept was based upon using idle cash value dollars and earning a modest seven percent return on an annuity. We would never suggest that a client use his cash value to invest in anything else—nor did he need to when a simple seven percent did so well. And the fact was that most people were not interested in getting involved in borrowing from their cash values and investing on their own. It sounded too complicated. That is, too complicated in a normal economy.

Remember my mentioning the great recession that hit just as we received approval to sell Columbia Life stock? Poor timing. Now here I was ten years later looking at an economy that all of a sudden was paying 18 percent on certificates of deposit. People began to realize that it was a good deal for them to borrow their cash values on their own. We would make presentations and explain how the leveraging of money worked and then show our illustration with a low interest rate, and once they understood, they also understood that they could use that money to better advantage than we could—for the moment.

All at once we had ten agents not making a living and we were going in the hole $9,000 a month from administrative salaries and rent. We struggled for nine long months hoping the economy would get reasonable. Reaganomics was killing us. Finally we threw in the towel. Gary went back to being a pharmacist. Doug went back to being a CPA. And I went back to my office at home— again—and thought about the $80,000 I personally owed the bank. Thank goodness I still had some equity in my home. I refinanced, paid off everything, and started all over again. What great growing experiences I was having!

Almost simultaneously, Universal Life hit the marketplace. Agents were showing illustrations of this exciting new product with a 16 percent estimated return, and they were blowing whole life proposals right out of the water. Mass replacement of permanent policies started taking place. An agent didn't need to have selling skills in order to make a living—just replacement skills. And, since many companies did not like the idea of paying a commission for changing a policy from Whole Life to Universal Life in their own company, many agents began switching their clients to other companies to earn a new commission while looking for anybody with permanent policies which could be switched to their companies. A lot of new commissions were being paid without new premiums being created. That, in my eyes, was not a positive.

Agents who preferred to keep their clients in Whole Life were sometimes forced to suggest changing just to protect themselves. If they didn't suggest changing, somebody else would—and the proposals for Universal Life, for the moment, looked too good not to change. I wonder just how many policyholders around the United States changed policies in the hopes of making a 14 percent or 15 percent return that never materialized. Too many, I fear.

I was caught in a trap. I just didn't like Universal Life. I suspect I was being a bit stuffy about it. Yet, what was I to do? I had a lot of policyholders out there who were just ripe for another agent to pluck.

Another "damned if I do and damned if I don't" situation.

The problem resolved itself when an agent friend of mine, Jeff Elgin, suggested to me that he call on my clients and explain Universal Life and at least offer them the option to change—something I just didn't want to do.

The result was that my clients were given the opportunity to compare their present program with

Universal Life, and given the pros and cons of changing. Not all of the resulting changes worked out, over time, as I would have liked.

Jeff and I split any resulting commissions, and for the next two years, along with the income from my Alpha seminars, I was able to stay almost even with my significant cash flow requirements.

However, I was setting myself up for another fall. I was not creating many new clients, and I was running out of old clients for Jeff to call on.

Finally, I had to refinance my house again. I had gone from a $60,000 mortgage on it 10 years earlier to a whopping $246,000. My monthly payment was now $2,600 and that along with other expenses was putting enormous pressure on me to produce. I missed the good old days when I was meeting new people, visiting with clients and selling life insurance. Why couldn't I just do that again? Maybe the size of my monthly obligations was paralyzing me.

While facing these professional and financial challenges, a tragedy of immense proportions was taking place in our family. My sweet Gloria had been diagnosed with Alzheimers disease in 1980 at the age of fifty-one. This is not the place to go into what all of us went through, but germane to this book was the fact that I now had to have full time, live-in help to care for her. Even more threatening than the expenses involved was the thought that it would not be too long before my Gloria would have to be cared for in a nursing home. I was not sure how I would be able to face the inevitable.

And—the financial specter was frightening. With the projected nursing home expenses, my mortgage, and office overhead, I was facing an annual bill of $75,000 before I could even put food on the table.

I was as close to financial disaster as I could get, but I just couldn't seem to pull myself up. I was using up assets just to live on. I sold my 1965 Mercedes which I had restored. I hated to part with it, but I needed cash. I did the same with several other things.

Finally, I had to go to the savings and loan that held the mortgage on my house and explain that I was going to have a tough time making the monthly payments and if they would be patient I would put my home on the market and pay them off just as soon as it sold. They weren't happy, but neither was I.

Again, poor timing seemed to be on my side. The real estate market was depressed. Our dream home which we had built in 1970 was a beautiful 5,000 square feet, used brick, French Country house and it was worth over $300,000 in any decent market. My luck was not to have it so. The savings and loan had been patient, but they could no longer go along. I had to get the house sold—now— and I would have to take the first offer or lose the house. The first offer was for $212,000 and I had no choice but to sell. Since my mortgage amounted to $246,000, the savings and loan agreed to reduce the amount I owed them by a bit and take most of our beautiful antiques at the appraised value and a personal note for the balance. They were more than fair.

Since I left Columbia Life, my net worth had increased to $725,000 due mostly to the appreciation of our home, our antiques, and another piece of property. Now I had lost it all. I was left with a net worth of $30,000, and a note that would take me five more years to pay off. My lessons had been learned.

It finally occurred to me that being just a traditional

life insurance salesman, with no business responsibilities to anyone except my clients, was the sweetest deal in the world. Sure, it was still the worst paid easy work—but it was also still the best paid hard work. The good news was that I knew how to work hard. I made the decision to go back to doing what I knew best—making phone calls, setting up appointments, uncovering problems and offering solutions.

I would do it in a manner that offered quality of life. And—I definitely would never again forget the lesson, of keeping perspective and balance in life, shared with me by Grant Taggart.

Reflections

*A*s I review the foregoing chapter and think about that era in my life, I realize that it would be very easy for you to view many of the circumstances as negative. And you would be right. However, the insight I gained from these experiences helped me to learn:

> *I cannot always control my circumstances,*
> *but I can always control my reaction*
> *to those circumstances.*

I learned that *my attitude belongs to me* and that no person or event can control it without my permission. From that understanding evolved the next step:

> *I may not pick the circumstances,*
> *but by maintaining a positive outlook,*
> *I will learn the lessons being offered and*
> *grow into a better person.*

I believe it was Earl Nightingale who said something like "In every adversity lies the seed of a bigger and better success." I believe this with all my heart.

If it were not for the ups and downs of my

experiences, I do not believe my first book, *From the Heart of a Child,* nor this book, would have been written. Positive results can evolve from negative situations.

Circumstances not to your liking or your choice are going to come to you. That's life! My wish for you is that you find the power to step outside of yourself and look for the lessons to be learned— and then learn them with a positive expectancy for the future. That's living!

> *"It's not what happens to you,*
> *It's what you do about it."*

> W. Mitchell

"*There is more to life*
Than faster."

Inspired by Gandhi

CHAPTER 24

Back To Basics

I had finally come full circle. Agent to president to general agent and back to agent. I contacted my long time friend, and agency manager for the Standard Insurance Company, Barney Rogers and said, "How would you like to have another agent with a fair amount of experience in your agency?" Barney said, "Who?" And I said, "Me!"

I had finally learned that the grass is *not* always greener on the other side.

I didn't need to set any more records. I had done that. I would never again measure success in numbers that kept asking for an answer to "How much is enough?" I would never again lose sight of the importance of balance in all areas of life.

And, I didn't need to prove I was okay I had discovered we are all okay And starting all over again financially was also okay. I had proved that when the effort is made, the results are assured.

My thinking about what was necessary to create a great life had changed. I didn't need my restored Mercedes, or my Lincoln Continental. I didn't need my dream home. I missed it but it was alright that it was gone. Gloria and I had raised our family there and it had served its purpose beautifully.

I now knew that:

There are more important things in life than running on the treadmill, faster and faster.

Being of great service, even to a few, adds significantly to one's life purpose.

Status is a poor substitute for quality of being.

And that:

People are more important than things.

But I had learned something else that was equally important. I learned that my choice of opportunity versus security thirty-two years before had reaped a paradox. By choosing opportunity, I had gained security.

Sure I was broke. So what. That was only an inconvenience that would be rectified by what I had irrevocably gained. I owned ability, and knowledge, and courage. I knew how to uncover problems and offer solutions. I knew how to ask questions and listen for the answers. I knew how to put myself in the prospect's shoes and determine how I would want the problem solved if I were he. In essence:

I appeared to have lost everything, but I had not lost two of my most important assets—my positive attitude and my ability to uncover problems and offer solutions. I would gain back all that I wanted or needed because—

I had irrevocably earned the badge of a sales professional

What a tremendous feeling of freedom. I still called all the shots. I could determine the size of my income and the hours I would give to produce it. I could pick the kind of people I wanted to deal with, and make friends in the process.

Shortly after joining Barney's agency, the significance of my freedom was brought home to me. A close friend of mine had been working for a big corporation for about twenty five years, gathering his security around him like a cloak, until one day out of the blue he was "offered" early retirement. He still had ten more years before normal retirement and before his pension fund would be enough to support the lifestyle he and his wife hoped to maintain. There is no need to go into the trauma he experienced, but I can tell you that under no circumstances would I trade places with him. I had a bright future looking at me. He had dark clouds.

So, in spite of circumstances, I had a direction to head for. My talent was needed. There would always be a market for it. I didn't have to take over someone else's job. I had one waiting for me. I was a commodity, and I was in demand.

As I looked out toward what the future might hold,

I realized it was all up to me. I knew what I wanted in my insurance practice, and because of the freedom this would allow me, I began to create a new vision. In this vision I saw myself writing an inspirational book on life, and another on selling—and reaching out, through my books, and coaching, and speaking, to help others discover their path to success.

All these were possibilities for the future. It excited me. And these possibilities were only available for me because in October of 1952 I had voted for opportunity instead of security.

I give thanks!

Reflections

*A*s I reminisce over those first thirty-two years, I am drawn to talk about the life Gloria, our children and I enjoyed because of the insurance business.

Sometime in the early 1960s I gave a silver charm bracelet to Gloria, with silver charms representative of each place we had been on our insurance convention trips. On each future trip we purchased a charm to add to the bracelet.

I was looking at the bracelet the other day and a flood of memories came back. Our first ocean cruise, San Francisco to Honolulu on the Matsonia. Our experience of riding in an outrigger canoe off Waikiki beach when a big wave drove our bow into the sand and the stern came right on over the top of us. The time out of Mexico City when a guide we had hired took us searching for buried artifacts. He took us to this place among the ruins where it looked like the moles had been working overtime. Sure enough, we found artifacts—two days old. No tip for that guide!

I could go on and on, but the point is that we were experiencing some of the great places in the world because of the insurance business. Looking at the bracelet I tried to identify all the places we had been—not too successfully. I could recognize five charms from Hawaii, one from Portugal, one from Munich, and one from Lucerne—all separate trips. All in all, I calculated we travelled to about thirty major conventions at beautiful spots all over the world, taking the children with us many times.

The two greatest rewards over all those years were the freedom we felt—the freedom to make our own decisions, to make our own mistakes, to make our own money—and the friends we made, a list of which I'm sure would run close to a thousand.

What a great business where clients become friends and friends become clients. The best of all worlds.

I hope that every once in awhile you will step back and assess all the blessings that are yours because of this business. They may not seem very abundant now, but be patient. They are all out there waiting for you.

All you have to do is make some choices and leave your comfort zone behind. Just do it. It's really worth it.

"*Were it offered to my choice*
        I should have no objection
To a repetition of the same
        Life from its beginning, only
Asking the advantages author's
        Have in a second edition
To correct some faults in the first."

Benjamin Franklin

"*Here is a test to find whether*
Your mission on earth is finished.
If you're alive, it isn't."

Richard Bach

CHAPTER 25

Major Reflections

Today, as I write this chapter, it is October 1, 1992. Forty years ago this day I started my *Great Adventure*. If you were to ask me what I would do differently if I had it to do all over again, I'd have to reply, "How much time do you have?"

I would do a multitude of things differently. That's what life's lessons are all about. But if you were to ask me if I have any major regrets, I would have to answer, "Absolutely not!" My life has been so blessed in so many areas I can't imagine not having an attitude of thankfulness. And the fun I've had! I've enjoyed more handball, tennis, golf, skiing, and great friendships than anyone I know.

Sure, I would like to have had some things work out differently. It would have been nice to have the financial matters turn out more favorably since enough money in the bank is one of life's great freedoms. But look at it this way—that still gives me something to look forward to.

But would I trade even one of the adventures for more money? The answer is a definite *"No!"* Even the "Great Detour," Columbia Life, taught me valuable lessons that I would not have learned elsewhere.

On the other hand, if you were to ask what advice I could offer you, I might first refer you to the text of a talk David Marks gave at the 1971 MDRT meeting entitled "Shoemaker, Stick to Your Last." David's insightful message, in which he addressed the agent as a businessman, urged you to make your business your major investment. And to treat your business like a business. David quoted the economist Roger Babson who said, "Many men are well on the road to success. In some cases they are financially independent at age forty-five or fifty, but there is no particular distinction at being in this class because 90 percent of them will lose their entire accumulation before they are sixty-five due to the reinvestment hazard." The point is that many have made it in the sales profession, and then lost it by getting involved in investment opportunities they knew nothing about or were not suited for. I can vouch for that!

It's been almost nine years since I met with Barney Rogers and became part of his agency. I would like to tell you that once I concentrated on being an agent I always lived by all that I learned. I would like to, but I can't. I have a ton of knowledge that has not been transferred into wisdom. I'm not sure the reason for this, but I assume it is just part of what life is all about.

I didn't go out and try to set any more records in insurance sales. I had no interest in that. Even so, I closed some of the biggest sales of my life. More importantly, I met some more wonderful people.

As I reflect back over all the years between 1952 and now, there is one message that kept reoccurring throughout my successes and nonsuccesses. I would like to share it with you:

With an unconditional love of life and an Everything-is-going-to-work-out-okay attitude— Everything will work out.

As you are faced with challenges in the years to come, maintain a positive outlook and believe that things are turning out as they should. Because they are—and you will gain in wisdom. With that kind of an attitude, you can handle anything.

There is a Japanese proverb that says:

Fall seven times, stand up eight.

That is an attitude! That is *also* the secret to success in life!

"Take time to laugh
It is the music of the soul.
Take time to think
It is the source of power.
Take time to play
It is the source of perpetual youth.
Take time to read
It is the fountain of wisdom.
Take time to pray
It is the greatest power on earth.
Take time to love and be loved
It is a God-given privilege.
Take time to be friendly
It is the road to happiness.
Take time to give
It is too short a day to be selfish.
Take time to work
It is the price of success."

Anon

CHAPTER 26

Some Thoughts
For You

Years ago I came across one author's opinion of the *Twelve Great Riches of Life.* I can't give proper credit to the author, but here they are:

Positive Mental Attitude
Sound Physical Health
Harmony in Human Relationships
Freedom from Fear
Hope of Achievement
The Capacity for Faith
Financial Security
A Labor of Love
An Open Mind on All Subjects
Self-discipline
The Capacity to Understand Other People
The Willingness to Share One's Blessings

As you look at this list, realize how lucky you are that your profession gives you the opportunity to pursue each and every one of these "riches."

You are in control of you and your life as a commissioned sales person. How much money you make, how much fun you have, and how many people you serve, is directly up to you.

You also have more opportunity to grow than the average person. You have to take more risks, face more rejection, ask more questions, listen for more answers, come up with more solutions. Count your lucky stars.

There may be times, however, when you will feel like crying out, "Oh no! Not another growing experience." But in the end, you will appreciate that each challenge is just one more stepping stone on the path.

I hope you will always remember that successfully facing challenges and striving to be the best you can be at your profession is only one goal in your life. You should also have a soul goal. Every day you should strive to be the very best you can be in all areas of your life. You have that opportunity—and that responsibility.

So step outside of yourself every now and then and assess what is going on. Is your life satisfying in the big picture? Did you just have your best sales week, but failed to make time for your family, your body, your mind, your friends, or your God? Be aware, imbalance is an insidious thief of what's important.

Everything that *really* counts in life is either invisible or free. Friendships, nature, a beautiful sunset, love, peace of mind, energy, enthusiasm, faith—these and like blessings are what really matter.

Because you have chosen the path of opportunity, you also have chosen *Freedom!* The freedom to create your own destiny. The freedom to make a difference. And, most importantly, the freedom to:

Believe in all that you are and
become all that you can become.

And so, as we come to the end of this book, let me wish for you a vision of the masterpiece within you just waiting to be created. Pick up the brush and touch it to the canvas. You have places to go, people to see, and things to do.

And all it takes is—

The Heart of a Lion!

For when the one great scorer comes
To write against your name,
He marks—not that you won or lost—
But how you played to game.

Grantland Rice
Sportswriter, 1880-1954

"All knowledge,
Unless committed to memory,
And put into action
Is useless."

Anonymous

A Call
To Action

I have started almost every seminar I've conducted for the past thirteen years by asking the audience to write down the quote on the opposite page. Unless new ideas become part of your daily life, they will wither and die. I have seen so many people, including myself, become excited about a new direction and then fail to take that first action step.

I hope you have discovered an idea or two while reading this book which may add value to your life. If so, now is the time for action. I have provided space at the end of the book for you to record any of the ideas you might like to work on. My title is "Action Ideas." You may prefer to use another title, but it is important to put your ideas into writing. It is the first step.

As you grow your list will change and expand. My

goal is to give you a reference point to remind you of who you are and where you're going.

Also, when you do take an idea and make it work, let me hear from you. I would enjoy learning about your victory.

At the end of most *Reflections* there is a one-liner for you to think about. Here are some additional "Points to Ponder." They are a call to action.

Tell your whole family about your goals,
And make sure they receive rewards
When you accomplish them.
Your family makes a great cheering section.

Your children are only with you for a short time—
Don't ever be too busy for them.

If your clients could remember what they bought
And why they bought it, they wouldn't need you.
They won't remember—and they do need you.

Remember, your prospect doesn't care how much you know
Until he knows how much you care.

If a competitor has already done a good job for a prospect,
Congratulate the prospect and compliment the competitor.

Don't worry about competition—
You are the only one you need to compete with.

If you're making money for the glory of making money—
You're losing the game.

It's people, not numbers that make you a success.

The best salesperson asks the best questions.

Know what you want to say.
Ad lib is for amateurs.

Keep everything simple.
You already know how smart you are,
And others don't care.

Make a friend out of every client.
It adds value for both of you.

To set sales records and miss your child's ballgames is
Baloney
To set sales records and ignore your health is
Baloney
To set sales records and ignore your spiritual side is
Baloney

Don't take minor adversities to heart.
If an event is not going to have a major negative impact
On you life five years from now—let it go.

Refuse to measure your self-worth
By how much business you do,
Or how much money you earn.

You are already a diamond.
Life just gives you the opportunity to do some polishing.

You're as good as they get—once you believe it.

Mediocrity in any area of life can lead to unhappiness.

Happiness is the pursuit of excellence.

Always reach for the stars—that is why they are there.

If you want to change,
Do something differently—Now!

All the knowledge in the world won't take the place
Of stepping up to bat and taking a swing.

Action is the secret ingredient to all change.

You don't quit playing because you grow old—
You grow old because you quit playing.

And remember:

The good things in life are the mortal enemy
Of the great things in life.

Isn't it time to go for the Great Things?

Good Luck and God Bless!

Action Ideas

"What I hear—I forget.
What I see—I remember.
What I do—I understand."

Confucius

1. _____
2. _____
3. _____
4. _____
5. _____
6. _____
7. _____
8. _____
9. _____
10. _____
11. _____
12. _____
13. _____
14. _____
15. _____

In Appreciation ... Thank You

How do I go back forty years and possibly pay homage to all the people who have touched my career? I want to thank everyone, but it is an impossible task. Nevertheless, at the risk of overlooking someone, I do want to mention the following:

All my competitors from my town of Albany in those early years. Especially Bob Mikkelson, George Chambers, Bob Jacobson and Bill Sprague. They were always gentlemen and I hope they believe I returned the favor.

Raymond Fisher, Bert Harger and Jim Metzker for their inspiration, guidance and encouragement.

The founding members of the Willamette Association of Life Underwriters. Each played some part in what I learned.

Bob Cummins whose belief in me was the catalyst for my grabbing my boot straps.

The folks at Western Life who stuck by me. Especially Orson Kelly, Luther Thompson, Gale Linebarger and Chuck Bradham. Plus four presidents— Bob Richardson, Tom Patterson, Bill Johnson, and Ralph Young. My favorite sales vice-president Bob Utne. Bruce Barnett who was always there at those special times I needed help. And all the agents from Western Life who were a source of learning and inspiration.

The agents in Oregon and around the United States who are more than just friends. They are part of who I am today.

The members of the MDRT and guest speakers at the annual meetings who have shared their light and made the way brighter for the rest of us. I would like to mention just a few of the many who by their words, their example, or their individual help, have made my life better:

Ben Feldman	Frank Sullivan
Tom Wolff	John Todd
Jim Longley	Dr. Carl Symington
Dr. Victor Frankl	John Savage
Dr. Maxwell Maltz	Jim Harding
Dr. Hans Selye	Dave Hilton
Bruce Jenner	Hank McCamish
Joe Sorrentino	Millard Grauer
Dr. Alec Mackenzie	Buzzy Budnitz
Bob Gallivan	Prudy Harker
Jim Rice	Lyle Blessman
Norm Levine	Karl Bach
Denis Waitley	Al Prewitt
John Utz	Al Granum
Rosanne LaFlamme	Con Demas
Nate Kaufman	Roger Zener
Larry Wilson	Charlie Flowers
Mark Schooler	Mun Charn Wang
Tom Thorkelson	

Capt. Gerald Coffey USN (Ret.)

About The Author

Bill O'Hearn's career includes 40 years in the life insurance industry as agent, general agent and president of a life insurance company. In 1980 he founded the Alpha Learning Institute for the purpose of delivering the message of human potential through seminars and lectures. Bill, a proud grandfather of five, resides in Oregon with his wife, Elizabeth, where he pursues life as a speaker, consultant, golfer, skier and outdoor enthusiast.

From The Heart Of A Child - And Other Lessons To Live By was his first book.

From The Heart Of A Lion - And Other Lessons To Sell By is his second book.

• • •

Bill O'Hearn is a member of the National Speakers Association and is available for:

- Speeches
- Keynotes
- Workshops
- Seminars

To schedule him for your organization's most important event(s), please call:

503-694-2255
or
800 537-9991

More Bill O'Hearn *Resources*

Order Form

Books	Price	Quantity	Total
From The Heart Of A Lion	11.95	_____	_____
From The Heart Of A Child	11.95	_____	_____
Tapes			
Relaxation	6.95	_____	_____
Relaxation with Affirmations	6.95	_____	_____
Spread Your Wings And Fly	6.95	_____	_____
Shipping/Handling (1-2 books)	2.50	_____	_____
Each additional book	1.00	_____	_____
Each tape)	1.00	_____	_____
Total Order		_____	_____

Name: _____

Address: _____

City/State/Zip: _____

Phone; Bus.: _____ Home: _____

If paying with credit card, please complet information below:

[ ] Visa   [ ] MasterCard

_____	_____	_____
Card #	Expiration Date	Your Signature

Please return this order form with check or money order payable to:

Entheos Publishing Company
P.O. Box 970
Willsonville, Oregon 97070

TO ORDER TODAY CALL
503-694-5800 or 800-537-9991